Linking Wilderness Research and Management

Volume 1– Wilderness Fire Restoration and Management:

An Annotated Reading List

Series Editor

Vita Wright
Research Application Program Director
Aldo Leopold Wilderness Research Institute
Rocky Mountain Research Station
U.S. Department of Agriculture, Forest Service
Missoula, MT 59807

Author

Marion Hourdequin
Graduate Research Assistant
Duke University
Durham, NC 27705
(formerly with the Aldo Leopold
Wilderness Research Institute)

USDA Forest Service
General Technical Report RMRS-GTR-79-vol. 1.

September 2001

Preface

Federal land management agencies have recognized the importance of incorporating the best available scientific knowledge into management decisions. However, both managers and researchers have struggled to identify effective processes for accomplishing this objective. The Aldo Leopold Wilderness Research Institute's Research Application Program works toward understanding barriers to the use of science in management and developing ways to make relevant scientific information more accessible. Managers can base their decisions on the best available scientific knowledge only if they are aware of current and relevant science as well as how it fits into their management goals.

The Linking Wilderness Research and Management series of annotated reading lists was developed to help land managers and others access scientific information relevant to protecting and restoring wilderness and similarly managed lands, as well as the myriad of values associated with such lands. References in these reading lists have been categorized to draw attention to the relevance of each publication, and then organized to provide a logical framework for addressing the issue. Each volume begins with references necessary to understand the overall issue, and then provides references useful for identifying management goals, understanding influences on those goals, and finally, for selecting and implementing management approaches. For example, the Fire Restoration and Management volume begins with sections on general fire ecology and anthropogenic effects, then covers the history and goals of wilderness fire management, and finishes with sections addressing management approaches, options, and considerations and constraints. Within each section, articles have been annotated to clarify their relevance to that section and to highlight their relevance to wilderness management.

These reading lists were designed to serve a wide audience. First, each list introduces generalists to the breadth of factors that should be considered when addressing a management issue. These volumes also enable specialists to maintain familiarity with research relevant to their discipline but outside their area of expertise. For instance, the Invasive Plants volume may be useful to a botanist who specializes in protecting rare species but is not familiar with the invasive plant literature. For those generally familiar with the concepts, this series facilitates access to literature that can add depth to their conceptual knowledge. Rather than produce comprehensive bibliographies, which may be unwieldy for those with limited time, the authors included overviews, the most current examples of literature addressing pertinent concepts, and frequently cited classic publications. These lists can provide a starting point for readers interested in more detail on specific subjects to conduct their own literature reviews.

To facilitate access to these lists and enable us to update them, the lists are also available through the Aldo Leopold Wilderness Research Institute's Web site (http://www.wilderness.net/leopold). The Leopold Institute is a Federal interagency research institute that focuses on ecological and social science research needed to sustain wilderness ecosystems and wilderness values. I hope this series will help sustain wilderness, similarly managed lands, and associated values by enabling managers, policymakers, educators, user groups, and others to access the best available science on the topics covered.

—Vita Wright, *Series Editor*

Acknowledgments

We wish to thank Robert Keane, Peter Landres, Caroline Lansing, Carol Miller, David Parsons, and Catherine Stewart for reviews and helpful comments on the manuscript. We appreciate David Ausband's and Alison Perkins' help with proofreading, and thank the interagency Aldo Leopold Wilderness Research Institute, the interagency Arthur Carhart National Wilderness Training Center, and the Rocky Mountain Research Station for their sponsorship of this project.

Contents

INTRODUCTION

Humans have long maintained a complex and dynamic relationship with wildland fire. While native North Americans utilized fire for hundreds of years to promote growth of certain plants, facilitate hunting, and clear travel corridors (Williams 1994), during most of the 20th century fire on U.S. public lands was viewed as dangerous and destructive. For decades, Federal agencies have worked to suppress and minimize wildland fire on public lands, including wilderness and other similarly protected areas (Parsons and Landres 1998). To protect scenery and natural features, for example, early National Park managers worked to save these areas from destruction by fire (Parsons and Botti 1996). Yet ecological research gradually revealed that fire plays a more complex role in ecosystems than we previously believed (Christensen 1988). Although it is true that fire changes landscapes, many of these changes help to maintain mosaics of vegetation, recycle nutrients, and conserve biological diversity (Kilgore 1986). Additionally, anthropological research has shown that humans have not always had an adversarial relationship with fire, and that in fact, fire played an important role in the hunting and gathering systems of many Native American tribes (Lewis 1985).

In light of this understanding, fire management on U.S. Federal lands has changed. Rather than attempt to suppress all fires, managers now work to minimize the risks associated with fire while allowing fire to play a more natural role in maintaining ecological processes and communities (NPS and others 1998). Permitting a natural role for fire is particularly appropriate for wilderness and protected areas with the mandate to maintain natural conditions; however, restoring fire to ecosystems after decades of fire suppression poses many challenges (Parsons 2000). In many areas, the structure and composition of plant communities has changed in response to fire suppression. In the absence of fires, woody fuels tend to accumulate in forests, which in turn can increase their susceptibility to intense fires (Arno and others 2000). Additionally, due to population growth and development, many wilderness areas and National Parks now border homes or communities, increasing the risks associated with escaped fires. Restoring fire to wilderness and protected areas requires management that integrates ecological and social knowledge, taking into account the effects of various management options on plant, animal, and human communities.

A significant body of knowledge has developed surrounding fire ecology, fire management, and wilderness fire restoration. This knowledge draws on the experiences of managers in the field, as well as on the physical, natural, and social sciences. The literature collected here represents a small subset of this vast literature, selected for its relevance to the issue of wilderness fire restoration and management.

As a broad overview of the literature on wilderness fire, this reading list does not offer sufficient information on which to base fire management plans. Specific plans for restoring and managing fire in wilderness will require site-specific knowledge, because ecosystems are varied and complex. An understanding of local plant communities, their effects on fire behavior, and their responses to fire will be of central importance, as will information on animal distributions, behavior and habitat requirements, patterns of natural and human disturbance, jurisdictional boundaries, social and recreational values, and risks to life and property. Nonetheless, the structure of this reading list, and the papers we have cited and annotated, should provide readers with a conceptual framework for applying wilderness fire research to management. Furthermore, the reading list can help readers to identify the *types* of local and regional knowledge needed to manage fire in wilderness in accordance with the purposes set forth in the Wilderness Act and similar legislation designed to protect the values of naturalness and wildness on public lands.

SCOPE

This reference list provides an overview of key literature relating to fire restoration and management in wilderness and similarly protected areas. This list, which centers on the United States, should be helpful to managers or researchers new to the topic, or to those seeking knowledge about specific aspects of wilderness fire management. Because of the large volume of information on wildland fire, as well as the efforts of other agencies and research organizations to synthesize this information, we did not develop a comprehensive bibliography on all aspects of fire ecology and management. Instead, we focus on the scientific literature that relates most directly to wilderness fire issues. We have given particular attention to the challenges of returning fire to wilderness following a history of fire suppression.

The reading list emphasizes recent literature over older papers and favors papers with a broad geographic and scientific scope over those that are narrower. We focus on recent literature because Federal land management agencies have mandates to utilize the "best available science," which usually means the most current research, and because newer papers tend to cite important older works, enabling the reader to pursue these. A few older classic papers are included, however, where they provide the best source for concepts important to current research and management.

We chose to emphasize geographical and topical breadth because we intend the reference list to provide a starting point for reading and research—to outline "the lay of the land" for wilderness fire restoration, and to be useful to managers throughout the United States. Region- and site-specific information and details about specific techniques are crucial to effective fire management, but including such information would diminish the list's effectiveness as a manageable outline of key general references. Additionally, although we strived for geographical balance, a substantial portion of the literature on wilderness fire restoration comes from the Western United States, and the list reflects this geographical concentration.

We have tried not to duplicate other efforts to compile fire science for managers; instead we direct readers to existing databases or resources. For example, although fire modeling is an important aspect of wilderness fire management, we include few references on this topic, because the Fire Sciences Laboratory in Missoula, MT, serves as an excellent resource for technical advice regarding predictive fire models. Similarly, the Tall Timbers Research Station maintains an extensive, searchable bibliography on fire ecology. We have attempted to identify such relevant resources, and we refer readers to them in annotations throughout the reading list.

Although not comprehensive, the sources cited here represent a significant portion of the wilderness related fire literature. This reading list gathers together and organizes this literature in a way that we hope will be useful to both managers and researchers.

ORGANIZATION

The organizing outline for this reading list provides a framework for understanding and evaluating wilderness fire management options and their consequences. The list is divided into three parts. The first part provides background information that underpins fire management generally, including books and papers on fire ecology, fire as a natural disturbance, and human relationships with fire. The second part, which forms the core of the reading list, focuses specifically on fire restoration and management in wilderness and protected areas. Papers on the history and philosophy of wilderness fire set the context. Next, the list covers planning, management, and evaluation of wilderness fire programs, as well as the constraints on fire restoration. Many of the citations in this section examine strategies for returning fire to wilderness, in keeping with the Wilderness Act's mandate that in wilderness, natural processes should prevail. The third and final section lists additional resources—such as policy documents, online databases, and sample fire plans—relevant to wilderness fire restoration and management.

The reading list is further broken down by topic. Within each topic, the articles are alphabetized by author's last name. Major topics are prefaced by a paragraph introducing and summarizing the literature included within the section to orient the reader and highlight key papers. To avoid duplication, annotations for papers relating to multiple topics were included in the section we judged most relevant. However such papers are listed and cross-referenced in the other relevant sections as well.

REFERENCES

Arno, Stephen F.; Parsons, David J.; Keane, Robert E. 2000. Mixed-severity fire regimes in the Northern Rocky Mountains: consequences of fire exclusion and options for the future. In: Cole, David N.; McCool, Stephen F.; Borrie, William T.; O'Loughlin, Jennifer, comps. Wilderness science in a time of change conference—Volume 5: wilderness ecosystems, threats, and management; 1999 May 23–27; Missoula, MT. Proc. RMRS-P-15-VOL-5. Ogden, UT: U.S. Department of Agriculture, Forest Service, Rocky Mountain Research Station: 225–232.

Christensen, Norman L. 1988. Succession and natural disturbance: paradigms, problems, and preservation of natural ecosystems. In: Agee, James K.; Johnson, Darryll R., eds. Ecosystem management for parks and wilderness. Seattle, WA: University of Washington Press: 62–86.

Kilgore, Bruce M. 1986. The role of fire in wilderness: a state-of-knowledge review. In: Lucas, R. C., ed. Proceedings: national wilderness research conference: issues, state-of-knowledge, future directions; 1985 July 23–26; Fort Collins, CO. Gen. Tech. Rep. INT-220. Ogden, UT: U.S. Department of Agriculture, Forest Service, Intermountain Research Station: 70–103.

Lewis, Henry T. 1985. Why Indians burned: specific versus general reasons. In: Lotan, James E.; Kilgore, Bruce M.; Fischer, William C.; Mutch, Robert W., eds. Proceedings—symposium and workshop on wilderness fire; 1983 November 15–18; Missoula, MT. Gen. Tech. Rep. INT-182. Ogden, UT: U.S. Department of Agriculture, Forest Service, Intermountain Forest and Range Experiment Station: 75–80.

National Park Service; U.S. Department of Agriculture, Forest Service; Bureau of Indian Affairs; U.S. Fish and Wildlife Service; Bureau of Land Management. 1998. Wildland and prescribed fire management policy: implementation procedures reference guide. Boise, ID: National Interagency Fire Center.

Parsons, David J. 2000. The challenge of restoring natural fire to wilderness. In: Cole, David N.; McCool, Stephen F.; Borrie, William T.; O'Loughlin, Jennifer, comps. Wilderness science in a time of change conference—Volume 5: wilderness ecosystems, threats, and management; 1999 May 23–27; Missoula, MT. Proc. RMRS-P-15-VOL-5. Ogden, UT: U.S. Department of Agriculture, Forest Service, Rocky Mountain Research Station: 276–282.

Parsons, David J.; Botti, Stephen J. 1996. Restoration of fire in National Parks. In: Hardy, Colin C.; Arno, Stephen F., eds. The use of fire in forest restoration. Gen. Tech. Rep. INT-GTR-341. Ogden, UT: U.S. Department of Agriculture, Forest Service, Intermountain Research Station: 29–31.

Parsons, D. J.; Landres, P. B. 1998. Restoring natural fire to wilderness: how are we doing? In: Pruden, Teresa L.; Brennan, Leonard A., eds. Fire in ecosystem management: shifting the paradigm from suppression to prescription; 1996 May 7–10; Boise, ID. Tall Timbers Fire Ecology Conference Proceedings, No. 20. Tallahassee, FL: Tall Timbers Research Station: 366–373.

Williams, Gerald W. (1994.) References on the American Indian use of fire in ecosystems [Online]. Available: http://wings.buffalo.edu/academic/department/anthropology/Documents/firebib [2001, June 1].

ANNOTATED READING LIST

I. Fire Ecology and Management

A. Overviews

An understanding of fire ecology provides an important underpinning for wilderness fire management. The books, proceedings, and articles in this section offer key background on wildland and wilderness fire. Topics include fire behavior, fire effects on plants, animals, and ecological processes, fire regimes, and legal, policy, and management issues relating to fire. Two reviews (Agee 2000; Kilgore 1986) and a conference on wilderness fire (Brown and others 1995) discuss the unique issues involved in the science and management of fire in protected areas. The other publications focus more broadly, but contain useful background on fire science and various approaches to managing wildland fire.

Agee, James K. 1993. Fire ecology of the Pacific Northwest forests. Washington, DC: Island Press. 493 p.

Annotation: This book gives a thorough account of fire ecology in the Pacific Northwest United States. The first six chapters provide general background on the ecology of fire, including discussions of fire regimes, the cultural history of fire in North America, fire history methodologies, and fire's effects on plant communities. Examples are primarily from the Pacific Northwest, but these chapters offer a useful overview of fire ecology generally. The remainder of the book focuses on specific forest and ecosystem types of the Pacific Northwest, covering fire regimes, stand development patterns, fuels, and management issues.

Agee, James K. 2000. Wilderness fire science: a state of the knowledge review. In: Cole, David N.; McCool, Stephen F.; Borrie, William T.; O'Loughlin, Jennifer, comps. Wilderness science in a time of change conference—Volume 5: wilderness ecosystems, threats, and management; 1999 May 23–27; Missoula, MT. Proc. RMRS-P-15-VOL-5. Ogden, UT: U.S. Department of Agriculture, Forest Service, Rocky Mountain Research Station: 5–22.

Annotation: This paper reviews progress in wilderness fire science and management since Kilgore's 1986 review (see

annotation, this section). Agee documents an increased understanding of fire behavior and effects, as well as an improvement in fire models with the advent of GIS and other tools. However the lack of sufficient data to parameterize and test fire models—and specifically, the lack of weather information for wilderness—limits our ability to use predictive models in wilderness fire management. Additional work is also needed to incorporate patchiness and variability into simulations of fire behavior and effects. In addition to identifying these research and information needs, Agee traces the history of fire science and management in wilderness and protected areas and points to key books and proceedings on these topics. The review identifies three challenging areas for future work: understanding and managing fire in a landscape context, further improving our knowledge of fire behavior and effects, and integrating weather and climate change data into wilderness fire science.

Brown, James K.; Mutch, Robert W.; Spoon, Charles W.; Wakimoto, Ronald H., tech. coords. 1995. Proceedings: symposium on fire in wilderness and park management; 1993 March 30–April 1; Missoula, MT. Gen. Tech. Rep. INT-GTR-320. Ogden, UT: U.S. Department of Agriculture, Forest Service, Intermountain Research Station. 283 p.

Annotation: This conference proceedings contains a wide variety of papers about wilderness fire, written by both researchers and managers. Most papers relate directly to fire management and represent many different angles, including ecological science, communication and public relations, compliance with Federal laws and regulations, and funding. Most of the papers are short and free of technical jargon. The volume provides a good overview of key issues relating to fire and protected areas.

DeBano, Leonard F.; Neary, Daniel G.; Ffolliott, Peter F. 1998. Fire's effects on ecosystems. New York: John Wiley and Sons. 333 p.

Annotation: This recent textbook provides an overview of fire behavior and fire effects on ecosystems and relates this information to fire management. The book includes a brief summary of each section (Fire Dynamics, Soil Responses, Responses of Other Resources, and Management Implications), and the chapters are broken into subcategories, allowing the reader to reference specific topics. Although not focused specifically on protected areas, the book considers a variety of topics relevant to wilderness fire management, including a detailed section on fire effects on cultural resources. Other pertinent topics include discussions of planning prescribed burns and the role of fire in ecosystem restoration. Also, the discussion of soil and belowground effects of fire sets this book apart from other similar texts.

Hardy, Colin C.; Arno, Stephen F., eds. 1996. Proceedings: the use of fire in forest restoration: a general session at the annual meeting of the Society for Ecological Restoration; 1995 September 14–16; Seattle, WA. Gen. Tech. Rep. INT-GTR-341. Ogden, UT: U.S. Department of Agriculture, Forest Service, Intermountain Research Station. 86 p.

Annotation: This proceedings contains papers relating to needs assessment for fire restoration, restoration of fire in inland forests, and restoration of fire in Pacific Westside forests. The themes of structural and process restoration unite many of the contributions.

Kilgore, Bruce M. 1986. The role of fire in wilderness: a state-of-knowledge review. In: Lucas, R. C., ed. Proceedings: National wilderness research conference: issues, state-of-knowledge, future directions; 1985 July 23-26; Fort Collins, CO. Gen. Tech. Rep. INT-220. Ogden, UT: U.S. Department of Agriculture, Forest Service, Intermountain Research Station: 70–103.

Annotation: This thorough review outlines wilderness fire research and relates this information to management. Kilgore discusses fire history, effects, and behavior, reviews research methods and findings in these areas, and shows how fire research has been applied to park and wilderness management. In addition, the paper points out ongoing controversies in wilderness fire management and identifies research needs. The paper heavily cites the literature and references many classic studies from throughout the United States, Canada, and Australia. Although written nearly two decades ago, the paper remains a useful resource on the topic of wilderness fire.

Nodvin, Stephen C.; Waldrop, Thomas A., eds. 1991. Fire and the environment: ecological and cultural perspectives: proceedings of an international symposium; 1990 March 20–24; Knoxville, TN. Gen. Tech. Rep. SE-69. Asheville, NC: U.S. Department of Agriculture, Forest Service, Southeast Forest Experiment Station. 429 p.

Annotation: This proceedings covers a broad range of topics relating to wildland fire and its management. Subtopics covered in the proceedings include fire ecology, fire management, cultural issues, fire history, and the Yellowstone fires of 1988. Although not all of the papers relate directly to wilderness fire, a number of the studies focus on National Parks, and a variety of key ecological, policy and social issues are discussed.

Pyne, Stephen J.; Andrews, Patricia L.; Laven, Richard D. 1996a. Introduction to wildland fire—second edition. New York: John Wiley and Sons. 769 p.

Annotation: This book provides an overview of fire science and management. The first part discusses the fundamentals of wildland fire, covering fire behavior, fuels and weather. The second section emphasizes fire regimes, fire ecology, and fire history and provides an introduction to fire management. Fire management is the exclusive focus of the third section, which includes detailed discussions of fire suppression and prescribed fire. The final section, concerning fire around the world, offers an international perspective. Although the subject of wilderness fire does not play a prominent role in the book, the topics covered are relevant to all fire management, and a number of case studies deal with fire in parks and wilderness areas. Additionally, each chapter concludes with a section on further readings to assist the reader in pursuing specific topics.

Tall Timbers Research Station. (Ongoing). E. V. Komarek Fire Ecology Database. Available: http://www.talltimbers.org/feco.html [2001, June 1].

Annotation: This extensive, online, keyword-searchable database includes more than 10,000 articles relating to the ecology and management of fire. The database draws on scientific papers, books, conference proceedings, and agency documents and is international in scope, though weighted somewhat toward the Southeastern United States. The database is updated continuously and is free to access.

Whelan, Robert J. 1995a. The ecology of fire. New York: Cambridge University Press. 346 p.

Annotation: Whelan provides an overview of the ecology of fire, emphasizing population and community level effects. The book covers basics of "the phenomenon of fire," then turns to fire's effects on individuals and populations of animals and plants. The influence of fire on community characteristics such as species richness and composition are also considered. Whelan closes with a chapter on fire management, which describes the challenges of applying ecological theory to management and attempts to overcome some of those challenges by relating the information from earlier chapters to practical issues faced by managers. Included is a section on hazard reduction burning and its ecological implications, as well as a discussion of prescribed fire which lists a number of questions useful in deciding how to restore fire to natural areas.

Whelan, Robert J. 1995b. Fire and management. In: Whelan, Robert J. The ecology of fire. New York: Cambridge University Press: 294–308.

Annotation: In this chapter, Whelan discusses the prospects for and barriers to ecologically-based fire management. Fire has been used by humans for centuries for a variety of utilitarian purposes with little attention to ecosystem-level effects, though we now have an improved understanding of the ecological role of fire. Lack of communication between scientists and managers and the dearth of management-related science act as barriers to the integration of ecology into fire management. Many fire programs emphasize hazard-reduction burning rather than natural fire regimes. Differences in the ecological effects of hazard-reduction burning versus natural fire are discussed. Whelan recommends the use of historical fire regimes to guide fire management, though he acknowledges limitations in fire history methodologies as well as disagreement about the goals of fire restoration. A list of considerations for natural fire management is included along with suggestions for research and monitoring for natural fire programs. The article contains information relevant to planning prescribed burning and to managing fire for "naturalness" rather than purely utilitarian goals.

B. Fire Behavior and Effects (Selected Reviews)

This section contains a number of recent papers on fire behavior and fire effects on plants, animals, landscapes, and aquatic ecosystems. In selecting papers, we emphasized reviews that synthesize a portion of the literature on these vast topics. For example, under fire behavior, Albright and Meisner (1999) review fire simulation systems and their use in fire management, while Turner and Romme (1994) discuss the relationship between landscape characteristics and fire behavior. In the realm of fire effects, Gresswell (1999) provides a discussion of aquatic systems, Johnson and Miyanishi (1995) examine the importance of fire behavior and effects in planning prescribed burns, McLoughlin (1998) looks at the effects of fire seasonality on plants and animals, Brown and Smith (2000) discuss fire effects on flora, and Smith (2000) synthesizes the literature on animals' responses to fire. In "Fire at the Landscape Scale," papers focus on spatial patterns of fire and landscape heterogeneity, and the reciprocal interactions between fire and landscape characteristics. Included throughout are references to more comprehensive information sources, such as the Fire Effects Information System compiled and maintained by the U.S. Forest Service Fire Sciences Laboratory in Missoula, MT. These resources may be particularly helpful to those seeking information on a specific species or aspect of fire effects and behavior.

1. Fire Behavior

Albright, Dorothy; Meisner, Bernard N. 1999. Classification of fire simulation systems. Fire Management Notes. 59(2): 5–12.

Annotation: This article provides an overview of fire behavior models and their uses. Albright and Meisner classify fire simulation systems as physical, physical-statistical, statistical, or probabilistic and explain the differences among these types. Additionally, techniques for simulating fire spread (for example, bond percolation, cellular automaton) are described. The paper also identifies key

considerations for managers selecting a fire simulation system and provides a brief description of six recent systems. The paper distills a substantial amount of technical information into a clear and accessible format, paying particular attention to the use of models in fire management.

Johnson, E. A.; Miyanishi, K. 1995. The need for consideration of fire behavior and effects in prescribed burning. Restoration Ecology. 3(4): 271–278.

Annotation: See annotation in section I.B.2, page 8.

Pyne, Stephen J.; Andrews, Patricia L.; Laven, Richard D. 1996b. Fire behavior. In: Pyne, Stephen J; Andrews, Patricia L.; Laven, Richard D. Introduction to wildland fire—second edition. New York: John Wiley and Sons: 46–89.

Annotation: This chapter provides a thorough overview of fire behavior. Different types of fire—ground fire, surface fire, and crown fire—are discussed, along with their relationships to fuels, topography, and weather. The chapter also covers fire growth, spread, and intensity, and fire modeling techniques. Pyne and others include case histories for a number of specific fires from the Western, Midwestern, and Southeastern United States, linking the fire behavior principles discussed in the chapter to specific management situations.

Turner, Monica G.; Romme, William H. 1994. Landscape dynamics in crown fire ecosystems. Landscape Ecology. 9(1): 59–77.

Annotation: This paper discusses factors that control crown fire behavior, with particular attention to landscape characteristics. Work in Yellowstone National Park and elsewhere illustrates that landscape features and crown fires influence one another: landscapes shape fire behavior and fire behavior shapes landscapes. Crown fires tend to occur in drought-prone areas, and they generate nonequilibrium dynamics, making it difficult to characterize "natural" fire regimes for these areas and posing a challenge for natural fire management. The paper points out that fire behavior is influenced by patterns and processes at multiple scales in space and time; therefore models that focus only on local scale processes may be inadequate to predict burning patterns, particularly for crown fires or fires that spread through "spotting."

www.fire.org. (2000, July 10–last update). Available: http://www.fire.org [2001, June 1].

Annotation: This Web site provides access to a number of tools and models currently available to help predict fire behavior. The site itself is more of a clearinghouse than a content-rich resource. However, it offers links to the BehavePlus, FARSITE, and FIREFAMILY+ fire prediction tools. In addition, the site links to both the Fire Effects Information System (FEIS, annotated below, section I.B.2) and the Citation Retrieval System, a keyword-searchable database of the scientific literature used in compiling the FEIS.

2. Fire Effects on Plants, Animals, and Ecological Processes

Agee, James K. 1993. Fire ecology of the Pacific Northwest forests. Washington, DC: Island Press. 493 p.

Annotation: See annotation in section I.A, page 5.

Brown, James K.; Smith, Jane Kapler, eds. 2000. Wildland fire in ecosystems: effects of fire on flora. Gen. Tech. Rep. RMRS-GTR-42-VOL-2. Ogden: UT: U.S. Department of Agriculture, Forest Service, Rocky Mountain Research Station. 257 p.

Annotation: This volume offers a thorough review of the scientific literature pertaining to wildland fire's effects on vegetation and fuels. Following an opening chapter which provides background on fire regimes, the report offers a detailed discussion of fire's effects on plants—how fire influences plant mortality, vegetative regeneration and regeneration by seed, and other aspects of plant growth and reproduction. Chapters three through seven examine fire effects on plants in five major North American ecosystems. The eighth chapter focuses on climate change interactions with fire, and the final chapter examines the relationship between ecological principles and fire management. Though the volume covers a vast literature, the organization of the chapters makes the information accessible and clear.

DeBano, Leonard F.; Neary, Daniel G.; Ffolliott, Peter F. 1998. Fire's effects on ecosystems. New York: John Wiley and Sons. 333 p.

Annotation: See annotation in section I.A, page 6.

Gresswell, Robert E. 1999. Fire and aquatic ecosystems in forested biomes of North America. Transactions of the American Fisheries Society. 128: 193–221.

Annotation: This review examines the effects of fire on biological and physical characteristics of aquatic ecosystems and identifies research needs relating to aquatic ecosystems and fire. Although fire can have both direct and indirect effects on nutrients, aquatic invertebrates, and fishes, these effects vary depending on watershed characteristics (for example, geomorphology, soils), pre- and postfire vegetation structure, climate, weather, and other factors. Additionally, fire interacts with the anthropogenic effects of land use history. Two detailed tables summarize the results of selected studies on the biological and physical effects of fires on forested watersheds. Although the author makes few generalizations about fire and aquatic systems, he does suggest that many aquatic species evolved with and are adapted to fire. However, postfire recovery of populations at the landscape scale requires connectivity and refugia that can act as sources for recolonization.

Haase, Sally M.; Sackett, Stephen S. 1998. Effects of prescribed fire in giant sequoia-mixed conifer stands in Sequoia and Kings Canyon National Parks. In: Pruden, Teresa L.; Brennan, Leonard A., eds. Fire in ecosystem management: shifting the paradigm from suppression to prescription; 1996 May 7–10; Boise, ID. Tall Timbers Fire Ecology Conference Proceedings, No. 20. Tallahassee, FL: Tall Timbers Research Station: 236–243.

Annotation: This study investigated the effects of prescribed burning on soil temperature, tree cambium temperature, and soil nutrients in giant sequoia-mixed forest in Sequoia and Kings Canyon National Parks. Although soil and cambium temperatures reached levels with the potential to damage sequoia trees, the authors recorded no mortality in giant sequoia. In contrast, sugar pine experienced significant mortality (67 percent). However, the authors suggest that regeneration of both sugar pine and giant sequoia after prescribed burning suggests that the loss of sugar pine is short term. Although the paper is specific to two tree species in the Sierra Nevada, the study highlights the potential effects of prescribed burning, and the indepth methods section may be useful in designing similar studies elsewhere.

Johnson, E. A.; Miyanishi, K. 1995. The need for consideration of fire behavior and effects in prescribed burning. Restoration Ecology. 3(4): 271–278.

Annotation: Johnson and Miyanishi argue in this paper that prescribed burn prescriptions should be based not on the goal of emulating "natural" or historic conditions, but rather on specific management goals related to fire effects. The paper reviews basic information on the process, behavior, and effects of fire, then discusses the applications of this information to setting fire objectives. Although the general approach described may not be consistent with wilderness and protected area management strategies, a number of Johnson and Miyanishi's recommendations—such as using site-specific, experimental techniques—may be helpful.

Leenhouts, Bill. 1997. Presettlement fire and emission production estimates: a framework for understanding potential system change. In: Bryan, D.C., ed. Conference proceedings—environmental regulation and prescribed fire: legal and social challenges. Tallahassee, FL: Center for Professional Development, Florida State University: 236–241.

Annotation: See annotation in section II.F.7, page 34.

McLoughlin, Lynette C. 1998. Season of burning in the Sydney region: the historical records compared with recent prescribed burning. Australian Journal of Ecology. 23: 393–404.

Annotation: Although this paper focuses on fire in the region surrounding Sydney, Australia, it addresses an issue of potential importance to North American fire management that has received little attention in the literature. McLoughlin first reviews studies of how the seasonality of fire affects plant and animal species. The paper then compares the seasonal distribution of recent prescribed fires near Sydney to the timing of fires during the early years of settlement (1788–1845). McLoughlin notes that the timing of fires has shifted away from spring and summer toward the winter months. Although the effects of this shift are not well understood, seasonality may have important ecological consequences, and more research is needed to understand the implications of replacing historic patterns of fire with prescribed burning during a different season.

Mooney, Harold A.; Bonnicksen, Thomas M.; Christensen, Norman L.; Lotan, James E.; Reiners, William A. 1981. **Fire regimes and ecosystem properties: proceedings of the conference**; 1978 December 11–15; Honolulu, HI. Gen. Tech. Rep. WO-26. U.S. Forest Service, Department of Agriculture. 594 p.

Annotation: See annotation in Section I.C.2, page 12.

Neary, Daniel G.; Klopatek, Carole C.; DeBano, Leonard F.; Ffolliott, Peter F. 1999. **Fire effects on belowground sustainability: a review and synthesis.** Forest Ecology and Management. 122: 51–71.

Annotation: This paper discusses the effects of fire on belowground processes. These processes in turn affect nutrient and water availability, and hence, plant growth, survival, and community composition. The effects of fire on biotic and abiotic processes in the soil are influenced by fire frequency and severity, both of which can be related to weather patterns and past management practices. Severe fires, which burn hot and move slowly, typically raise soil temperatures more than faster moving, less intense fires. Soil temperature plays an important role in determining fire effects on belowground sustainability. As temperatures rise above certain thresholds, nutrient volatilization and loss of organic matter occur, changes in soil physical characteristics take place, and soil organisms (bacteria, fungi, invertebrates) are killed. The authors point out that these changes influence soil nutrients and hydrology, which affect plant growth and community composition. Because plants in turn affect nutrient and organic matter inputs to the soil, fire-induced changes soil and plant communities can initiate feedback mechanisms that further modify soils. Throughout the paper the authors provide specific examples from the literature, emphasizing research from the Southwestern United States. Information on soil nutrients and organic matter, microbes, and soil vertebrates and invertebrates is discussed in separate sections, making the paper easy to navigate. In addition, the final section synthesizes existing information and identifies key research needs, calling for more work on the interactions among land use practices, fire, and belowground sustainability.

Russell, Kevin R.; Van Lear, David H.; Guynn, David C., Jr. 1999. **Prescribed fire effects on herpetofauna: review and management implications.** Wildlife Society Bulletin. 27(2): 374–384.

Annotation: This article reviews both the direct and indirect effects of fire on reptiles and amphibians, with an emphasis on literature and examples from the southeastern United States. The authors discuss behavioral responses to fire (for example, dispersal, burrowing) as well as research on fire's population-level impacts on herpetofauna. Most studies indicate that population effects are relatively small, and the authors suggest that the negative effects of prescribed fire on amphibian and reptiles (via direct mortality) may be outweighed by the benefits of prescribed fire for maintaining herptile habitat. The role of prescribed fire in shaping upland and aquatic habitats is discussed, with some attention to the role of burn season and intensity. The benefits, drawbacks, and uncertainties associated with the use of herbicides as a fire proxy are also outlined.

The authors conclude with a section on management implications and research needs.

Smith, Jane Kapler. 2000. **Wildland fire in ecosystems: effects of fire on fauna.** Ogden, UT: U.S. Department of Agriculture, Forest Service, Rocky Mountain Research Station; Gen. Tech. Rep. RMRS-GTR-42-VOL-1. 83 p.

Annotation: This technical report synthesizes the extensive literature on fire's effects on fauna. After an overview of fire regimes and historical patterns of fire in North American ecosystems, the report discusses fire's direct and indirect effects on animals at a variety of spatial and temporal scales. One chapter focuses exclusively on direct effects, identifying injury and mortality, escape and emigration, and immigration as three major responses to fire. The subsequent three chapters examine fire effects on animals at population, community, and landscape scales, and a fourth chapter emphasizes fire effects on wildlife foods. The report concludes with a discussion of management implications. Though birds and mammals are emphasized throughout, amphibians, reptiles and insects are also considered.

U.S. Department of Agriculture, Forest Service, Rocky Mountain Research Station, Fire Sciences Laboratory (2001, May). Fire Effects Information System, [Online]. Available: http://www.fs fed.us/database/feis/ [2001, June 1].

Annotation: This online database summarizes the literature on fire effects for approximately 900 plant species, 100 animal species, and 16 Kuchler vegetation types of North America. For each species and vegetation type, the database provides basic background information (for example, geographical distribution, ecological characteristics) and summarizes the scientific literature regarding the relationship between the species or vegetation type and fire. Additionally, references are listed for each species or vegetation type, allowing the reader to pursue individual studies on a particular topic of interest.

Whelan, Robert J. 1995a. **The ecology of fire.** New York: Cambridge University Press. 346 p.

Annotation: See annotation in section I.A, page 6.

3. Fire at the Landscape Scale

Baker, William L. 1992. **The landscape ecology of large disturbances in the design and management of nature reserves.** Landscape Ecology. 7(3): 181–194.

Annotation: See annotation in section I.C.1, page 10.

Baker, W. L. 1993. **Spatially heterogeneous multi-scale response of landscapes to fire suppression.** Oikos. 66: 66–71.

Annotation: See annotation in section I.D.2, page 14.

Lertzman, Ken; Fall, Joseph. 1998. **From forest scales to landscapes: spatial scales and the roles of disturbances.** In: Peterson, David L.; Parker, V. Thomas, eds.

Ecological scale: theory and applications. New York: Columbia University Press: 339–367.

Annotation: This chapter highlights the need to examine ecological disturbances at multiple scales. Using fire as an example throughout the chapter, the authors identify "seven lessons from stands to landscapes": key ideas for understanding disturbance regimes and landscape patterns at multiple scales and for understanding the relationships between small and large scale processes. Connections between ecological theory, empirical data, and land management are discussed throughout the chapter.

Sampson, R. Neil; Atkinson, R. Dwight; Lewis, Joe W. 2000. Mapping wildfire hazards and risks. [Co-published simultaneously as Journal of Sustainable Forestry, volume 11, numbers 1/2 2000.] New York: Food Products Press. 328 p.

Annotation: See annotation in section II.E, page 28.

Turner, Monica G.; Hargrove, William W.; Gardner, Robert H.; Romme, William H. 1994. Effects of fire on landscape heterogeneity in Yellowstone National Park, Wyoming. Journal of Vegetation Science. 5:731–742.

Annotation: See annotation in section II.F.4, page 32.

Turner, Monica G.; Romme, William H. 1994. Landscape dynamics in crown fire ecosystems. Landscape Ecology. 9(1): 59–77.

Annotation: See annotation in section I.B.1, page 7.

C. Fire as a Natural Disturbance

In recent decades, ecologists have learned that natural disturbance plays a key role in maintaining ecological processes, generating a mosaic of vegetation types, and providing diverse habitat for animal species. The papers in the first part of this section discuss ecological disturbances in a management context. Christensen (1989) applies ecological theory on disturbance to the management of wilderness, and Baker (1992) discusses how knowledge of disturbance regimes can be used to guide both the design and management of protected areas. Landres and others (1999) argue that management planning can incorporate natural disturbance by using the concept of natural variability.

Papers in the second part focus on fire regimes and how an understanding of fire patterns through time can guide management. Maruoka and Agee (1994) offer a brief summary of fire history methods and the different types of information they provide, while Moore and others (1999) and Swetnam and others (1999) discuss how historical reference conditions can be used in fire restoration planning. Other papers model the effects of fire management strategies over time (Baker 1993, 1994), compare recent fire patterns to historic regimes (Brown and others 1994; Fule and Covington 1999; Fule and others 2000), and compare historic and recent smoke emissions (Leenhouts 1997).

1. Ecological Disturbance and Ecosystem Management

Baker, William L. 1992. The landscape ecology of large disturbances in the design and management of nature reserves. Landscape Ecology. 7(3): 181–194.

Annotation: In this paper, Baker discusses the role of natural disturbance in the design and management of natural areas. Maintenance of natural disturbance regimes is recommended as a goal for nature reserves. However, reserve design typically has failed to take natural disturbance fully into account, emphasizing instead species habitat requirements. More research is needed to better understand disturbance attributes—particularly patterns of disturbance in space and time—and their effects on landscape structure, which in turn can assist in reserve design. The latter section of the paper discusses options for managing disturbance in natural areas, including the use of disturbance surrogates, suppression, and prescribed disturbances. Throughout the paper, the author uses examples involving fire.

Christensen, Norman L. 1988. Succession and natural disturbance: paradigms, problems, and preservation of natural ecosystems. In: Agee, James K.; Johnson, Darryll R., eds. Ecosystem management for parks and wilderness. Seattle, WA: University of Washington Press: 62–86.

Annotation: This paper provides a detailed history of plant succession paradigms and discusses fire and ecosystem management in light of our contemporary understanding of plant communities and how they change over time. Christensen contrasts the classical model of succession, where determinate patterns of community change lead to a stable, climax condition with recent work highlighting the complexity and diversity of successional patterns. Under the old model, plant communities were distinct entities, thus managers could focus on preserving representation of a number of distinct plant community types. Newer understanding, however, suggests that plant communities are not distinct but rather grade into one another. Additionally, natural disturbance has been found to play a key role in maintaining a diversity of plant communities at the landscape scale. The author emphasizes the importance of allowing or reintroducing natural disturbances such as fire in order to maintain landscape heterogeneity and ecosystem diversity.

Christensen, Norman L. 1989. Wilderness and natural disturbance. Forum for Applied Research and Public Policy. 4(2): 46–49.

Annotation: This short, nontechnical paper outlines changes in our understanding of ecological disturbance from the early 20th century to the present and describes the implications of these changes for wilderness management. Early ecologists viewed ecological succession as leading to a stable, climax state, whereas contemporary scientists view nature as constantly changing in response to natural disturbance. Under this latter, dynamic model, we should aim to preserve natural processes in parks and wilderness areas rather than focus on maintaining a particular static state. Christensen discusses the implications of the "patch dynamics" model for both reserve design and management.

Landres, Peter B.; Morgan, Penelope; Swanson, Frederick J. 1999. Overview of the use of natural variability concepts in managing ecological systems. Ecological Applications. 9(4): 1179–1188.

Annotation: This paper discusses the background and justification for using the concept of natural variability in setting natural resource management objectives. Natural variability, also referred to as "historic range of variability" and "natural range of variability," can set the context for management of fire and other disturbances in ecological systems. The authors discuss methods for assessing natural variability and applying this information to management. Incorporation of natural variability would move management toward greater flexibility and require adaptability in the face of surprise events. This flexibility can improve management, but also provides opportunities for abuse: the authors caution that natural variability should not be used to justify the large-scale substitution of resource extraction for natural disturbance in light of their different effects. A greater understanding of the historic role of natural disturbances can make natural variability a more effective tool for setting goals and predicting outcomes under different management regimes.

Lertzman, Ken; Fall, Joseph. 1998. From forest scales to landscapes: spatial scales and the roles of disturbances. In: Peterson, David L.; Parker, V. Thomas, eds. Ecological scale: theory and applications. New York: Columbia University Press: 339–367.

Annotation: See annotation in section I.B.3, page 9.

2. Fire Regimes: Research Methods and Management Implications

Agee, James K. 1993. Fire ecology of the Pacific Northwest forests. Washington, DC: Island Press. 493 p.

Annotation: See annotation in section I.A, page 5.

Baker, William L. 1992. The landscape ecology of large disturbances in the design and management of nature reserves. Landscape Ecology. 7(3): 181–194.

Annotation: See annotation in section I.C.1, page 10.

Baker, William L. 1993. Spatially heterogeneous multiscale response of landscapes to fire suppression. Oikos. 66: 66–71.

Annotation: See annotation in section I.D.2, page 14.

Baker, William L. 1994. Restoration of landscape structure altered by fire suppression. Conservation Biology. 8(3): 763–769.

Annotation: This paper presents the results of a simulation study of landscape disturbance by fire in the Boundary Water Canoe Area in Minnesota. Using a geographic information systems (GIS) model and historic fire data, Baker modeled two fire regimes—the actual historic regime for this area followed by fire restoration, and the fire regime in the absence of human settlement—examining the effects of each "treatment" on landscape structure. The model predicted a 50–75 year recovery time for certain landscape attributes (for example, mean patch shape) and much longer times (up to 250 years) for the recovery of other characteristics (for example, mean patch age). Baker points out that landscape recovery time will vary depending on the historical fire regime as well as the patterns of reintroduced fire. The limits of this type of simulation study are discussed, however models can be useful in predicting the effects of fire management policies over time.

Barrett, S. W.; Arno, S. F. 1982. Indian fires as an ecological influence in the Northern Rockies. Journal of Forestry. 80: 647–651.

Annotation: See annotation in section I.D.1, page 13.

Brown, James K.; Arno, Stephen F.; Barrett, Stephen W.; Menakis, James P. 1994. Comparing the prescribed natural fire program with presettlement fires in the Selway-Bitterroot Wilderness. International Journal of Wildland Fire. 4(3): 157–168.

Annotation: This study examines historical and recent fire regimes for the Selway-Bitterroot Wilderness of eastern Idaho and western Montana. Brown and others reconstructed presettlement fire histories based on fire scars and stand age classes, and the location and intensity of more recent fires (within the 12 years preceding the report) were mapped based on aerial photos, interviews with fire staff, overflights, and other data sources. Comparisons between historic and recent fire patterns show a lower fire frequency in recent years, despite a wilderness fire restoration program initiated in 1970. The authors suggest fire suppression as a likely contributor to this difference. The paper provides an example of how historical and contemporary fire regimes can be described, mapped, and compared, providing baseline information for wilderness fire restoration.

Brown, James K.; Bradshaw, Larry S. 1994. Comparisons of particulate emissions and smoke impacts from presettlement, full suppression, and prescribed natural fire periods in the Selway-Bitterroot Wilderness. International Journal of Wildland Fire. 4(3): 143–155.

Annotation: See annotation in section II.D.2, page 26.

Caprio, Anthony C.; Graber, David M. 2000. Returning fire to the mountains: can we successfully restore the ecological role of pre-European fire regimes to the Sierra Nevada? In: Cole, David N.; McCool, Stephen F.; Borrie, William T.; O'Loughlin, Jennifer, comps. Proceedings: wilderness science in a time of change—Volume 5: wilderness ecosystems, threats, and management; 1999 May 23–27; Missoula, MT. Proc. RMRS-P-15-VOL-5. Ogden, UT: U.S. Department of Agriculture, Forest Service, Rocky Mountain Research Station: 233–241.

Annotation: See annotation in section II.C.2, page 23.

Fule, Peter Z.; Covington, W. Wallace. 1999. Fire regime changes in La Michilia Biosphere Reserve, Durango, Mexico. Conservation Biology. 13(3): 640–652.

Annotation: This study compares historical fire regimes across a gradient of moisture and elevation in northern

Mexico's La Michilia Biosphere Reserve. The authors used fire scars to reconstruct fire history and identify recent changes in patterns of fire. Based on these data, Fule and others discuss general trends as well as the roles of site characteristics, climate, and human influences in La Michilia's fire regimes. The use of fire history and ecology in reserve planning and management is also considered.

Fule, Peter Z.; Heinlein, Thomas A.; Covington, W. Wallace; Moore, Margaret M. 2000. Continuing fire regimes in remote forests of Grand Canyon National Park. In: Cole, David N.; McCool, Stephen F.; Borrie, William T.; O'Loughlin, Jennifer, comps. Wilderness science in a time of change conference—Volume 5: wilderness ecosystems, threats, and management; 1999 May 23-27; Missoula, MT. Proc. RMRS-P-15-V-5. Ogden, UT: U.S. Department of Agriculture, Forest Service, Rocky Mountain Research Station: 242–248.

Annotation: This study describes fire history in three areas of Grand Canyon National Park from 1700–1997. The results are interpreted in terms of climate and historical changes in fire management. The authors discuss the relevance of presettlement fire data to current fire management and identify impediments to the reintroduction of fire in Grand Canyon National Park.

Maruoka, Kathleen R.; Agee, James K. 1994. Fire histories: overview of methods and applications. Tech. Notes BMNRI-TN-2. Technical Notes from the Blue Mountains Natural Resources Institute. OR: Blue Mountains Natural Resources Institute. 5 p.

Annotation: This note provides a concise overview of fire history methodologies and their utility in various situations. Point frequencies and area frequencies can each be used to reconstruct historic fire patterns, though they provide information at different spatial scales. Point frequencies are generally preferable in areas with low-intensity fire regimes, while area frequencies function better for areas with stand-replacing fires. Area frequencies can be used in calculating both the natural fire rotation and the fire cycle. Thorough fire histories generally depend on a combination of stand ages and fire scar sampling; techniques for collecting and analyzing fire scars are discussed. Finally, the paper briefly explains how fire history information can be applied to fire management and planning of prescribed fire.

McLoughlin, Lynette C. 1998. Season of burning in the Sydney region: the historical records compared with recent prescribed burning. Australian Journal of Ecology. 23: 393–404.

Annotation: See annotation in section I.B.2, page 8.

Mooney, Harold A.; Bonnicksen, Thomas M.; Christensen, Norman L.; Lotan, James E.; Reiners, W. A. 1981. Fire regimes and ecosystem properties: proceedings of the conference; 1978 December 11–15; Honolulu, HI. Gen. Tech. Rep. WO-26. U.S. Department of Agriculture, Forest Service. 594 p.

Annotation: Although this symposium proceedings is two decades old, it contains a variety of papers by prominent ecologists on the interactions between fire regimes and ecosystem properties. The first section includes overviews of fire regimes and their effects on northern ecosystems, western forests and shrublands, grasslands, southeastern ecosystems, and the tropics. In the second section, plant adaptations and responses to fire are discussed. The third part emphasizes the relationship between fire and ecosystem properties such as biogeochemical cycles, geomorphic process, and hydrology. The final section examines fire management options in light of ecological understanding and public policy.

Moore, Margaret M.; Covington, Wallace W.; Fule, Peter Z. 1999. Reference conditions and ecological restoration: a southwestern ponderosa pine perspective. Ecological Applications. 9(4): 1266–1277.

Annotation: This paper outlines the concepts of reference conditions and the evolutionary environment and explains their relationship to ecological restoration, using southwestern ponderosa pine forests as an example. Moore and others discuss the need to select and prioritize key ecosystem components in determining reference conditions, then illustrate how reference conditions can be used to plan restoration targets and techniques. The authors also point out the need for site-specific approaches and the importance of considering both ecological and social conditions in planning restoration. The paper is relevant to wilderness fire management because the examples involve southwestern protected areas with altered fire regimes, and the potential differences in restoration goals for wilderness versus Federal public lands generally are discussed.

Pyne, Stephen, J.; Andrews, Patricia L.; Laven, Richard D. 1996a. Introduction to wildland fire—second edition. New York: John Wiley and Sons. 769 p.

Annotation: See annotation in section I.A, page 6.

Swetnam, Thomas W. 1993. Fire history and climate change in giant sequoia groves. Science. 262: 885–889.

Annotation: See annotation in section II.F.6, page 33.

Swetnam, Thomas W.; Allen, Craig D.; Betancourt, Julio L. 1999. Applied historical ecology: using the past to manage for the future. Ecological Applications. 9(4): 1189–1206.

Annotation: This paper discusses both the utility and limitations of historical ecology in relation to land management and ecological restoration. The authors discuss the strengths and weaknesses of both natural (for example, tree rings, pollen, packrat middens) and documentary (for example, historical photos, maps, diaries) data sources. Both source reliability and sampling methods are critical in developing ecological histories, and multiple lines of data are recommended. The article includes a case study of historical vegetation composition and fire regimes in the Southwestern United States and describes its relevance to ecological restoration. The authors conclude that historical ecology can provide context for contemporary land management, reveal the variables that drive natural disturbance, and assist in the development of predictive fire models.

Taylor, A. H. 2000. Fire regimes and forest changes in mid and upper montane forests of southern Cascades,

Lassen Volcanic Park, California, U.S.A. Journal of Biogeography. 27: 87–104.

Annotation: In this study, Taylor investigated fire regimes and forest structure in mid- and upper-montane forests in northern California's Lassen Volcanic Park. Forest composition was found to vary with elevation and soil moisture, and fire regimes varied with forest composition and elevation. Additionally, changes in both forest composition and fire regimes occurred following the initiation of fire suppression in 1905. Taylor discusses the implications of these changes for management, and in particular for the reintroduction of fire to Lassen Volcanic and other National Parks.

D. Anthropogenic Effects on Fire Regimes

Humans have interacted with fire for thousands of years, and these interactions have varied widely from time to time and place to place. Wilderness management provides a paradigm for human interaction with fire, but one that generally emphasizes minimal interference with ecological processes. Yet wilderness managers today face the challenge of actively restoring fire to reverse the influences of U.S. fire suppression throughout the 20th century. To define an appropriate management paradigm for wilderness fire, it is helpful to consider how humans have interacted with fire in the past, how land use practices such as grazing have affected fuels and fire regimes, and how wilderness fire restoration might affect ecological systems through influences on habitat structure, plant communities, and forest insects and disease. The papers in this section discuss Native Americans' historical use of fire (Arno 1985; Barrett and Arno 198; Boyd 1999; Lewis 1985) and the relevance of Native American fire use to wilderness management (Vale 1993), the effects of fire suppression on ecosystems (Arno and Brown 1991; Arno and others 2000; Baker 1992, 1993; Keeley and others 1999), and other ecosystem changes associated with fire and anthropogenic effects.

1. Native American Burning

Arno, Stephen F. 1985. Ecological effects and management implications of Indian fires. In: Lotan, James E.; Kilgore, Bruce M.; Fischer, William C.; Mutch, Robert W., eds. Proceedings—symposium and workshop on wilderness fire; 1983 November 15-18; Missoula, MT. Gen. Tech. Rep. INT-182. Ogden, UT: U.S. Department of Agriculture, Forest Service, Intermountain Forest and Range Experiment Station: 81–86.

Annotation: In this short paper, the author reviews Indian fire use in a variety of North American vegetation types from the Great Plains to the Pacific Coast. In each case, the ecological effects of historical burning as well as the effects of management following European settlement are discussed. Arno then discusses the implications of Indian fire practices for park and wilderness management. Un-

derstanding the historical role of fire in specific ecosystems may assist managers in predicting vegetation responses to different fire regimes. Additionally, managers may in some cases seek to restore presettlement fire regimes and simulate Native American burning. However, the justification for substituting prescribed fire for Native American burning hinges on the definition of "natural" and clarification of management direction for protected areas.

Barrett, S. W.; Arno, S. F. 1982. Indian fires as an ecological influence in the Northern Rockies. Journal of Forestry. 80: 647–651.

Annotation: Barrett and Arno used both fire scar sampling and interviews with descendants of Native Americans and European settlers to characterize fire history in western Montana from the time prior to European settlement (pre-1860) to late 20th century. Mean fire intervals and interviews suggested that burning by Native Americans was frequent prior to fire suppression, which began circa 1910. Some areas, such as accessible valley bottoms, were burned more frequently than remote sites. Details of these findings and their implications for forest and wilderness management are discussed.

Boyd, Richard. 1999. Indians, fire and the land in the Pacific Northwest. Corvallis, OR: Oregon State University Press. 313 p.

Annotation: According to editor Robert Boyd, "the papers in this volume summarize virtually everything that is known about Pacific Northwest Indian use of fire in the environment" (p. 4), though he admits that much information has been lost as elders and their oral histories have died. The book provides a number of studies of Indians and fire in the Pacific Northwest, taking account of the geographical and cultural variation in fire use practices. Because the studies are grounded in diverse disciplines (anthropology, history, botany, and forestry), the book documents the relationships between Indians, fire, and ecological change from multiple perspectives. Though not directly tied to wilderness, the book may provide a historical and cultural context for contemporary fire management, particularly in the Pacific Northwest.

Lewis, Henry T. 1985. Why Indians burned: specific versus general reasons. In: Lotan, James E.; Kilgore, Bruce M.; Fischer, William C.; Mutch, Robert W., eds. Proceedings—symposium and workshop on wilderness fire; 1983 November 15–18; Missoula, MT. Gen. Tech. Rep. INT-182. Ogden, UT: U.S. Department of Agriculture, Forest Service, Intermountain Forest and Range Experiment Station: 75–80.

Annotation: In this paper, Lewis points out that Native American burning cannot be fully understood apart from its larger cultural context. Anthropological research has shown that indigenous people utilized fire not in isolation, but as one element of their hunting and gathering practices. Lewis illustrates this point with an example from the tribes of northern Alberta. Next the author turns to the implications of Native American fire use for contemporary park and wilderness management. Because native people used fire in conjunction with a variety of land management techniques, emulating Native American burning alone—without hunting, for example–may cause unexpected or undesired effects. Park planners seeking to reintroduce fire may benefit by consulting with anthropologists knowledgeable about the context in which fire was historically used.

Vale, Thomas R. 1998. The myth of the humanized landscape: an example from Yosemite National Park. Natural Areas Journal. 18(3): 231–236.

Annotation: This paper challenges the idea that pristine wilderness is a mere construct based on a Eurocentric notion of North America as uninhabited prior to European colonization. Using Yosemite National Park as an example, Vale argues that many landscapes, particularly in the West, were *not* manipulated intensively by Native Americans on a broad scale. In Yosemite, Vale suggests that human influences were concentrated in the valley, while higher mountainous areas were relatively unaffected by humans. Studies of historical fire regimes suggest that natural ignitions were responsible for much of the fire activity in Yosemite; Native American influences on fire may have been minimal and concentrated in particular areas. Vale suggests neither the idea of pure, pristine wilderness nor that of a fully humanized landscape captures the complexity of historical ecosystems. Empirical studies are needed to sort out where and how humans historically influenced the land.

Williams, Gerald W. (1994). References on the American Indian use of fire in ecosystems, [Online]. Available: http://wings.buffalo.edu/academic/department/anthropology/Documents/firebib [2001, June 1].

Annotation: This resource briefly summarizes research on fire use by Native Americans and lists more than 200 references from ecology, anthropology, history, geography, and archaeology relating to this topic. The overview identifies 11 ways in which Native Americans employed fire. These include hunting, crop management, improved growth and yields, fireproofing, insect collection, pest management, warfare, economic extortion, clearing of travel corridors, felling trees, and clearing of riparian areas. These motivations are addressed in the articles listed in the reading list, which range from reports written by 19th century European settlers to recent research findings on American Indians' use of fire.

2. Fire Suppression

Arno, Stephen F.; Brown, James K. 1991. Overcoming the paradox in managing wildland fire. Western Wildlands. 17(1): 40–46.

Annotation: This article discusses the paradox created by efforts to protect natural resources by suppressing fire. The authors suggest that decades of fire suppression have, in many wildlands, placed resources at risk. Focusing primarily on natural areas outside of wilderness, Arno and Brown explain how fire suppression can affect vegetation structure and fire processes in areas with different fire regimes. Historical fire suppression strongly affects managers' options for maintaining or restoring fire as a "natural ecosystem process." This task is further complicated by adjacent lands management, residential development in and around wildlands, and limited funds. Opportunities to restore natural fire regimes using prescribed natural fire and manager-ignited fire are discussed, considering constraints that vary from place to place and time to time.

Arno, Stephen F.; Parsons, David J.; Keane, Robert E. 2000. Mixed-severity fire regimes in the °Northern Rocky Mountains: consequences of fire exclusion and options for the future. In: Cole, David N.; McCool, Stephen F.; Borrie, William T.; O'Loughlin, Jennifer, comps. Wilderness science in a time of change conference—Volume 5: wilderness ecosystems, threats, and management; 1999 May 23–27; Missoula, MT. Proc. RMRS-P-15-VOL-5. Ogden, UT: U.S. Department of Agriculture, Forest Service, Rocky Mountain Research Station: 225–232.

Annotation: In this paper, Arno and others describe the typical consequences of fire suppression in areas with mixed-severity fire regimes. These consequences include declines in fire-dependent species such as ponderosa pine, increased dominance by uniform, single-aged stands, increased basal area, and greater tree density. The authors use areas of the Bob Marshall Wilderness that historically experienced mixed-severity fire regimes to illustrate changes under fire suppression. Possible fire restoration strategies for wilderness—particularly wilderness areas characterized by mixed-severity fire regimes—are then discussed and evaluated in light of their ecological effects, their consistency with wilderness values, and their practicality.

Baker, William L. 1993. Spatially heterogeneous multiscale response of landscapes to fire suppression. Oikos. 66: 66–71.

Annotation: In this paper, Baker describes a simulation study designed to examine the effects of fire suppression on landscape attributes in the Boundary Waters Canoe Area Wilderness of Minnesota. Using a GIS-based model, Baker simulated both historical fire regimes (with suppression beginning in 1911) and presettlement fire regimes (no suppression) from 1868 to 2368. The author presents the results of each simulation treatment at various spatial scales, pointing out how landscape heterogeneity varies depending on the scale of analysis. The implications of suppression-induced landscape changes for animal species are discussed. However, Baker cautions that attributing landscape change to fire suppression is difficult, given a variety of other factors (for example, grazing practices) that can also alter landscapes and vegetation structure. Baker concludes by suggesting that only a spatially explicit approach to prescribed burning can mitigate suppression effects without simply creating additional disturbance. Because such an approach requires detailed understanding of how landscape patches have been affected by fire suppression, the author recommends that prescribed burning programs proceed with caution, particularly in parks and wilderness areas.

Baker, William L. 1994. Restoration of landscape structure altered by fire suppression. Conservation Biology. 8(3): 763–769.

Annotation: See annotation in section I.C.2, page 11.

Boucher, Paul F.; Moody, Ronald D. 1998. The historical role of fire and ecosystem management of fires: Gila National Forest, New Mexico. In: Pruden, Teresa L.; Brennan, Leonard A., eds. Fire in ecosystem management: shifting the paradigm from suppression to prescription; 1996 May 7–10; Boise, ID. Tall Timbers Fire Ecology Conference Proceedings, No. 20. Tallahassee, FL: Tall Timbers Research Station: 374–379.

Annotation: See annotation in section II.C.2, page 22.

Brown, James K.; Arno, Stephen F.; Barrett, Stephen W.; Menakis, James P. 1994. Comparing the prescribed natural fire program with presettlement fires in the Selway-Bitterroot Wilderness. International Journal of Wildland Fire. 4(3): 157–168.

Annotation: See annotation in section I.C.2, page 11.

Fule, Peter Z.; Heinlein, Thomas A.; Covington, W. Wallace; Moore, Margaret M. 2000. Continuing fire regimes in remote forests of Grand Canyon National Park. In: Cole, David N.; McCool, Stephen F.; Borrie, William T.; O'Loughlin, Jennifer, comps. Wilderness science in a time of change conference—Volume 5: wilderness ecosystems, threats, and management; 1999 May 23–27; Missoula, MT. Proc. RMRS-P-15-VOL-5. Ogden, UT: U.S. Department of Agriculture, Forest Service, Rocky Mountain Research Station: 242–248.

Annotation: See annotation in section I.C.2, page 12.

Keeley, Jon E.; Fotheringham, C. J.; Morais, Marco. 1999. Reexamining fire suppression impact on brushland fire regimes. Science. 284: 1829–1832.

Annotation: In this paper, Keeley and others scrutinize the assertions that fire size and intensity in California shrublands have increased in response to fire suppression. Based on an examination of fire history data, the authors found that although fire frequency increased over the course of the 20th century, fire size and intensity did not increase. The claims of increased fire size and intensity are based on faulty assumptions about changes in fire regimes. The authors point out that fire suppression appears to have had little effect on stand-replacing fire regimes in California shrublands. In contrast, many Western U.S. forests have experienced substantial changes in fire patterns under fire suppression. The results of this study suggest that the responses of different ecosystems to fire suppression may vary, and site-specific information is needed to understand the impacts of fire suppression on a particular area.

3. Other Interactions: Grazing, Exotic Species, and Insects

D'Antonio, Carla M. 2000. Fire, plant invasions, and global changes. In: Mooney, Harold A.; Hobbs, Richard J., eds. Invasive species in a changing world. Washington, DC: Island Press: 65–93.

Annotation: This chapter reviews what is known about the interactions between fire, exotic plants, and global change. D'Antonio points out that fire frequently facilitates plant invasions, although in some ecosystems it may hinder establishment and spread of exotic plants. Disturbance by fire may affect the rate of exotic plant invasion, and conversely, exotic plants may influence disturbance regimes. For example, in some areas the presence of some invasive plants increases the intensity and severity of fires as compared to historical conditions. Finally, fire and invasion may interact with land use and global climate change, although the specific nature of interactions involving global climate change is not well understood. Throughout the paper, D'Antonio both analyzes general patterns and provides specific examples, and the studies she reviews are summarized in tables and organized geographically.

Fule, Peter Z.; Covington, W. Wallace. 1999. Fire regime changes in La Michilia Biosphere Reserve, Durango, Mexico. Conservation Biology. 13(3): 640–652.

Annotation: See annotation in section I.C.2, page 11.

Hobbs, Richard J.; Huenneke, Laura F. 1992. Disturbance, diversity, and invasion: implications for conservation. Conservation Biology. 6(3): 324–337.

Annotation: In this paper, Hobbs and Huenneke discuss how disturbance affects ecological communities and their susceptibility to invasion by exotic species. Beginning from a theoretical perspective, the authors characterize disturbance as a complex phenomenon, varying in type, frequency, and intensity. Specific examples are then discussed, including how fire affects plant communities. In fire-dependent ecosystems, fire may be crucial to maintaining the diversity of plant communities, while fire suppression may alter community structure and composition. On the other hand, fire can facilitate invasion by exotic plants—and invasion, in turn, can alter disturbance regimes and community response to disturbance. This paper provides a thorough overview of the relationships between diversity and invasion, drawing primarily on examples from grasslands around the world.

Madany, Michael H.; West, Neil E. 1983. Livestock grazing-fire regime interactions within montane forests of Zion National Park, Utah. Ecology. 64(4): 661–667.

Annotation: This paper offers an example of how livestock grazing and fire can interact to alter vegetation structure and composition and to change disturbance frequency. Comparing two ungrazed mesas in Zion National Park to a nearby, grazed plateau, the authors found that although both areas had ponderosa-pine dominated overstory, the understory of the grazed area was dominated by woody species such as pine, juniper, and oak, whereas the ungrazed understory was largely composed of herbaceous plants. With less herbaceous cover, the grazed areas became less susceptible to fire and recruitment of woody plants increased. Although grazing effects observed here may not be generalized to all ecosystem types, this study provides an example of how an anthropogenic factor can significantly alter forest structure and fire regimes.

McCullough, Deborah G.; Werner, Richard A.; Neumann, David. 1998. Fire and insects in northern and boreal forest ecosystems of North America. Annual Review of Entomology. 43: 107–127.

Annotation: This paper discusses the ways in which fire and insects can interact, providing examples of how fire regimes can affect insect diversity and insect outbreaks and conversely, how defoliating insects can alter forest structure and composition and change susceptibility to fire. The use of fire to control insects, the sometimes analogous effects that insects and fire have on succession, the effects of fire suppression on insect population dynamics, and the ways in which fire can alter insect community composition and diversity are each discussed. Although the paper emphasizes a particular geographical region—northern and boreal forests—the section on fire suppression may be helpful to those interested in wilderness fire restoration and how changes in fire regimes can alter insect dynamics, which in turn may affect both forest structure and patterns of fire.

II. Restoring and Managing Wilderness Fire

A. History of Wilderness Fire Management

Fire management in wilderness has changed significantly during the past century. After the dramatic fires of 1910, Federal public lands policy shifted strongly toward fire suppression. The goal of preventing fires from "damaging" ecological systems reflected the prevailing scientific theory of the time, which emphasized the development of ecosystems to a stable, climax state. As ecologists began to question the "balance of nature" paradigm and develop new views of ecosystems as dynamic, the use of fire suppression to preserve areas in a static state also came under scrutiny. In 1968, the National Park Service initiated a major change in policy, allowing lightning-caused fires to burn within the bounds of specific prescriptions and permitting manager-ignited prescribed fire (Parsons and Botti 1996). Other major Federal land management agencies with wilderness jurisdiction also have modified their policies to accommodate fire as a natural disturbance, although fire suppression continues to play a major role. The articles in this section examine the history of fire wilderness management and discuss policy changes over the course of the last century.

Agee, James K. 2000. Wilderness fire science: a state of the knowledge review. In: Cole, David N.; McCool, Stephen F.; Borrie, William T.; O'Loughlin, Jennifer, comps. Wilderness science in a time of change conference—Volume 5: wilderness ecosystems, threats, and management; 1999 May 23–27; Missoula, MT. Proc. RMRS-P-15-VOL-5. Ogden, UT: U.S. Department of Agriculture, Forest Service, Rocky Mountain Research Station: 5–22.

Annotation: See annotation in section I.A, page 5.

Brown, James K.; Mutch, Robert W.; Spoon, Charles W.; Wakimoto, Ronald H., tech. coords. 1995. Proceedings: symposium on fire in wilderness and park management; 1993 March 30–April 1; Missoula, MT. Gen. Tech. Rep. INT-GTR-320. Ogden, UT: U.S. Department

of Agriculture, Forest Service, Intermountain Research Station. 283 p.

Annotation: See annotation in section I.A, page 5.

Christensen, Norman L. 1991. Wilderness and high intensity fire: how much is enough. 1991. In: High intensity fire in wildlands: management challenges and options; 1989 May 18–21; Tallahassee, FL. Tall Timbers Fire Conference Proceedings No. 17. Tallahassee, FL: Tall Timbers Research Station: 9–24.

Annotation: This keynote address focuses on the relationship between ecological science and fire management throughout the 20th century. Christensen discusses the changing views of ecological succession and stability from the classical view of succession to climax to the contemporary paradigm of complexity and change. These changes are reflected in the management of wildland fires: under the classical view, fires and other disturbances were to be avoided in order to maintain stable, climax communities, whereas the modern view suggests that change is inherent in natural systems and fire maintains important ecological processes. Specific implications of this paradigm shift for the management of wilderness fire are discussed.

Christensen, Norman L. 1995. Fire and wilderness. International Journal of Wilderness. 1(1): 30–34.

Annotation: In this paper, Christensen discusses the evolution of parks and protected area management in relation to fire. When parks were first established in the late 19th century, they were viewed as "museums" to be preserved in a static condition. In recent decades, however, ecologists and managers began to recognize that natural systems are dynamic, and to adjust management to take change into account. Fire management policies have shifted from suppression to restoration of "natural" disturbance regimes using both natural and planned ignition fires. However, restoring fire has not been easy: ecological change is complex, and clear goals are needed to guide management.

And even when goals and management plans are set, we should "expect the unexpected," since we lack complete knowledge or control. Management that adapts in response to new information from research or monitoring will be most successful in achieving goals.

Parsons, David J.; Botti, Stephen J. 1996. Restoration of fire in National Parks. In: Hardy, Colin C.; Arno, Stephen F., eds. The use of fire in forest restoration. Gen. Tech. Rep. INT-GTR-341. Ogden, UT: U.S. Department of Agriculture, Forest Service, Intermountain Research Station: 29–31.

Annotation: This paper discusses the evolution of National Park Service fire management from attempting to suppress all fires to understanding fire as a natural process. Parsons and Botti trace the development of prescribed natural fire and prescribed burning programs in the National Parks, evaluate their success, and identify a number of challenges facing contemporary managers of fire in parks and other natural areas. These challenges include clarifying goals and objectives, integrating scientific research into management, working with limited resources, and cooperating across agency and administrative boundaries.

Parsons, David J.; Landres, Peter B. 1998. Restoring natural fire to wilderness: how are we doing? In: Pruden, Teresa L.; Brennan, Leonard A., eds. Fire in ecosystem management: shifting the paradigm from suppression to prescription; 1996 May 7–10; Boise, ID. Tall Timbers Fire Ecology Conference Proceedings, No. 20. Tallahassee, FL: Tall Timbers Research Station: 366–373.

Annotation: This paper discusses the evolution of fire restoration in wilderness, and evaluates the current situation on Federal lands. After briefly outlining the history of fire management in wilderness managed by the National Park Service (NPS), Forest Service (USFS), Bureau of Land Management (BLM), and the Fish and Wildlife Service (USFWS), the authors evaluate the accomplishments of each agency's fire program. The National Park Service currently has the most complete fire management records. However, wilderness is not separated from nonwilderness in NPS documentation. The three other agencies (USFS, BLM, USFWS) have poor or incomplete records, or have made little use of prescribed natural fire. The authors conclude with a number of recommendations, including better record keeping, increased coordination among agencies, improved integration of science, and explicit goals and standards for fire restoration.

B. Philosophy and Goals of Wilderness Fire Management

Wilderness and similarly protected areas are guided by unique philosophies that generally emphasize natural conditions and processes and aim to minimize human impacts. Thus, active management of fire in wilderness presents a dilemma: is it possible to reintroduce fire without "trammeling" wilderness? The articles in this section wrestle with philosophical questions such as this, which play an important role in setting wilderness management goals. For example, is it acceptable to manipulate wilderness vegetation in the short term to achieve longer term objectives of restoring fire as a natural process (Landres and others 2000; Sydoriak and others 2000)? And on a more practical level, should managers begin by reintroducing fire as a process, or should vegetation structure be restored to some historical condition before initiating prescribed burns (Agee and Huff 1986)? What types of goals should guide wilderness fire management (Barrett 1999; Bonnicksen and Stone 1985; Kilgore 1985)? Although they offer few definitive answers, the papers in this section raise important issues for consideration and elucidate some of the philosophical issues related to restoration of wilderness fire.

Agee, James K.; Huff, Mark H. 1986. Structure and process goals for vegetation in wilderness areas. In: Lucas, R. C., ed. Proceedings—National Wilderness Research Conference: current research; 1985 July 23–26; Fort Collins, CO. Gen. Tech. Rep. INT-212. Ogden, UT: U.S. Department of Agriculture, Forest Service, Intermountain Research Station: 17–25.

Annotation: This paper lays out a variety of ecological and philosophical considerations associated with wilderness fire management goals. The authors separately address goals for areas with frequent, intermediate, and infrequent fire, illustrating the importance of site characteristics in determining appropriate goals and methods. Specific examples from a variety of forest types are discussed, and the authors portray the complexity of wilderness fire management, taking into account factors such as the relationship between fire and insect infestation, the role of climate in driving vegetation change and fire, and the effects of fire suppression on both vegetation structure and disturbance processes.

Barrett, Stephen W. 1999. Why burn wilderness? Fire Management Notes. 59(4): 18–21.

Annotation: In this article, Barrett draws on his own fire history studies in central Idaho wilderness in asserting that recent fire patterns differ significantly from historical regimes in this region. Recent fires tend to be more intense and less frequent than those prior to 1900, and Barrett argues that their effects likely differ as well. Human influences have modified natural patterns and processes in wilderness, therefore human actions—in the form of prescribed fires—are needed to restore these patterns and processes. Barrett argues that simply leaving wilderness alone, as some advocate, will lead to species declines and the perpetuation of "mutant ecosystems of our own making."

Bonnicksen, T. M.; Stone, E. C. 1985. Restoring naturalness to the National Parks. Environmental Management. 9: 479–486.

Annotation: Fire management in National Parks suffers from a lack of quantitative standards by which to measure naturalness, according to Bonnicksen and Stone. The majority of National Parks are guided by legislation that directs managers to maintain natural conditions—but without clear standards, it is impossible to evaluate the effectiveness of park management. The authors assert that prescribed burning programs have been broadly applied in the parks of California's Sierra Nevada without well-defined goals.

Defining goals requires a better understanding of ecological history and thorough descriptions of historic stand structure that include spatial patterns. Bonnicksen and Stone argue that to restore natural fire processes and natural fire effects, vegetation structure may require manipulation in advance of reintroducing fire.

Brown, James K.; Mutch, Robert W.; Spoon, Charles W.; Wakimoto, Ronald H., tech. coords. 1995. Proceedings: symposium on fire in wilderness and park management; 1993 March 30–April 1; Missoula, MT. Gen. Tech. Rep. INT-GTR-320. Ogden, UT: U.S. Department of Agriculture, Forest Service, Intermountain Research Station. 283 p.

Annotation: See annotation in section I.A, page 5.

Kilgore, Bruce M. 1985. What is "natural" in wilderness fire management? In: Lotan, James E.; Kilgore, Bruce M.; Fischer, William C.; Mutch, Robert W., tech. coords. Proceedings—symposium and workshop on wilderness fire. Gen. Tech. Rep. INT-182. Ogden, UT: U.S. Department of Agriculture, Forest Service, Intermountain Forest and Range Experiment Station: 57–67.

Annotation: In this paper, Kilgore explores the concept of "natural" in managing wilderness fire, drawing both on the literature and on a survey of scientists and managers. The term "natural" has been interpreted in multiple ways, and ambiguity surrounds its definition. Can human-set fires be natural? Does natural fire management entail replicating historical fire patterns and effects, or allowing fire to evolve as a dynamic part of an ecosystem? Kilgore discusses a variety of responses to the question of naturalness, then concludes that natural fires are those that burn within the range of variability and cause the range of effects found prior to European technological influence.

Landres, Peter B.; White, Peter S.; Aplet, Greg; Zimmermann, Anne. 1998a. Naturalness and natural variability: definitions, concepts, and strategies for wilderness management. In: Kulhavy, David L.; Legg, Michael H., eds. Wilderness and natural areas in Eastern North America: research, management, and planning. Nacogdoches, TX: Stephen F. Austin State University, Arthur Temple College of Forestry, Center for Applied Studies: 41-50.

Annotation: The Wilderness Act charges managers with maintaining natural conditions—but what is natural, and how do we manage for naturalness? This article draws on ecology and the concept of historical range of variability to answer these questions. However, the authors acknowledge that science alone cannot define naturalness. The definition of naturalness depends on value judgments, which should be explicit and subject to debate. After providing a conceptual grounding, the authors describe a five-step strategy for managing natural areas for naturalness. Although the paper does not explicitly focus on fire, the concepts and framework are applicable to wilderness fire restoration and management.

Landres, Peter B.; Brunson, Mark W.; Merigliano, Linda; Sydoriak, Charisse; Morton, Steve. 2000. Naturalness and wildness: the dilemma and irony of managing wilderness. In: Cole, David N.; McCool, Stephen F.; Borrie, William T.; O'Loughlin, Jennifer, comps. Wilderness science in a time of change conference—Volume 5: wilderness ecosystems, threats, and management; 1999 May 23–27; Missoula, MT. Proc. RMRS-P-15-VOL-5. Ogden, UT: U.S. Department of Agriculture, Forest Service, Rocky Mountain Research Station: 377–381.

Annotation: In this paper, Landres and others discuss two primary goals of wilderness management, naturalness and wildness, grounded in the 1964 Wilderness Act. Especially as protected areas experience alterations caused by human actions outside of wilderness, the goals of naturalness and wildness come into conflict. It is no longer possible simply to "leave wilderness alone" and expect natural conditions to prevail. Landres and others identify tradeoffs between managing for naturalness and wildness, and discuss a case study from the Bandelier Wilderness in New Mexico, posing a series of difficult questions relating to ecological restoration, including restoration of fire, in this area.

Parsons, David J. 1990. Restoring fire to the Sierra Nevada mixed conifer forest: reconciling science, policy, and practicality. In: Hughes, H. G.; Bonnicksen, T. M., eds. Proceedings of the first annual meeting of the Society for Ecological Restoration; [Date of conference unknown]; Madison, WI. University of Wisconsin, Madison: 271–279.

Annotation: See annotation in section II.C.2, page 23.

Parsons, David J.; Graber, David M.; Agee, James K.; van Wagtendonk, Jan W. 1986. Natural fire management in the National Parks. Environmental Management. 10(1): 21–24.

Annotation: In this paper, Parsons and others discuss the goals of park and wilderness fire management, arguing that managers should aim to restore "the unimpeded interaction of native ecosystem processes and structural elements." The authors reject the view that parks should be managed to maintain the landscape in a particular historical state. Interference with natural processes should be limited to situations involving a compelling reason to intervene (for example, to mitigate human impacts or protect life and property). Parsons and others explain the justification for their position and discuss its implications for fire restoration and issues related to historical burning by Native Americans.

Parsons, D. J.; van Wagtendonk, J. W. 1996. Fire research and management in the Sierra Nevada National Parks. In: Halvorson, William L.; Davis, Gary E., eds. Ecosystem management in the National Parks. Tucson, AZ: University of Arizona Press: 24–48.

Annotation: This paper reviews the history and interplay of fire management and fire ecology research in the Sierra Nevada National Parks. In addition, it outlines past and present challenges to restoring fire in these parks. Parsons and van Wagtendonk describe the development of both prescribed burning and prescribed natural fire programs in the parks, in conjunction with scientific research and monitoring. They discuss debates over fire management goals, and the controversy over restoring presettlement conditions versus reintegrating fire as a process. Finally, the authors identify obstacles to the restoration of fire in the Sierra

Nevada parks, which include: (1) developing criteria for prescribed burning; (2) determining goals (structure versus process, aesthetic versus ecological); (3) defining "natural"; (4) program evaluation; (5) applying research findings to management; and (6) communicating goals and accomplishments.

Stephenson, Nathan L. 1999. Reference conditions for giant sequoia restoration: structure, process, and precision. Ecological Applications. 9(4): 1253–1265.

Annotation: See annotation in section II.C.2, page 24.

Sydoriak, Charisse A.; Allen, Craig D.; Jacobs, Brian F. 2000. Would ecological landscape restoration make the Bandelier Wilderness more or less of a wilderness? In: Cole, David N.; McCool, Stephen F.; Borrie, William T.; O'Loughlin, Jennifer, comps. Wilderness science in a time of change conference—Volume 5: wilderness ecosystems, threats, and management; 1999 May 23–27; Missoula, MT. Proceedings RMRS-P-15-VOL 5. Ogden, UT: U.S. Department of Agriculture, Forest Service, Rocky Mountain Research Station: 209–215.

Annotation: This paper lays out a number of difficult questions surrounding wilderness restoration, touching on issues of restoration goals, appropriateness of restoration methods, and legislative mandates for (or against) wilderness restoration. The Bandelier Wilderness, where grazing and fire suppression have altered natural processes and contributed to soil erosion, is used as a case study. Rather than definitively answer the questions they pose, the authors portray the complexity of the situation in this New Mexico wilderness and discuss the possibilities of manipulating vegetation and reintroducing fire to restore natural conditions.

Whelan, Robert J. 1995b. Fire and management. In: Whelan, Robert J. The ecology of fire. New York: Cambridge University Press: 294–308.

Annotation: See annotation in section I.A, page 6.

C. Restoring Fire: Planning, Implementation, and Evaluation

Fire can be reintroduced to wilderness ecosystems in one of two ways. Especially in large wildernesses or protected areas, naturally ignited fires can be employed to restore natural conditions and processes. Formerly known as "prescribed natural fire," this strategy is now known as "wildland fire use" (National Park Service and others 1998)—although much of the literature on this topic reflects the earlier terminology. The second major strategy for restoring wilderness fire is through prescribed burning. A number of researchers (for example, Brown 1992–1993) advocate prescribed burning to supplement or substitute for natural fire, particularly where wilderness areas are small, where risks associated with escaped fires are great, or where the frequency of naturally ignited fires has been significantly reduced from historic levels. In some wilderness areas, such as Wyoming's Gros Ventre Wilderness (U.S.

Department of Agriculture 1996), a combination of wildland fire use and prescribed burning is used.

The papers in the first section address wildland fire and prescribed burning as fire restoration techniques and discuss the importance of minimal impact fire suppression (Mangan 1985; Mohr 1994). Although fire restoration is under way in many areas, suppression continues to play a significant role in wilderness (Parsons 1998–1999), especially in small wilderness areas or areas close to residential development. Papers in the second part discuss the assessment and evaluation of wilderness fire restoration and examine how wilderness fire restoration might be improved.

1. Approaches and Options: Wildland Fire, Prescribed Burning, and Minimum Impact Fire Suppression

Arno, Stephen F.; Brown, James K. 1991. Overcoming the paradox in managing wildland fire. Western Wildlands. 17(1): 40–46.

Annotation: See annotation in section I.D.2, page 14.

Arno, Stephen F.; Parsons, David J.; Keane, Robert E. 2000. Mixed-severity fire regimes in the Northern Rocky Mountains: consequences of fire exclusion and options for the future. In: Cole, David N.; McCool, Stephen F.; Borrie, William T.; O'Loughlin, Jennifer, comps. Wilderness science in a time of change conference—Volume 5: wilderness ecosystems, threats, and management; 1999 May 23–27; Missoula, MT. Proc. RMRS-P-15-VOL-5. Ogden, UT: U.S. Department of Agriculture, Forest Service, Rocky Mountain Research Station: 225–232.

Annotation: See annotation in section I.D.2, page 14.

Boucher, Paul F.; Moody, Ronald D. 1998. The historical role of fire and ecosystem management of fires: Gila National Forest, New Mexico. In: Pruden, Teresa L.; Brennan, Leonard A., eds. Fire in ecosystem management: shifting the paradigm from suppression to prescription; 1996 May 7–10; Boise, ID. Tall Timbers Fire Ecology Conference Proceedings, No. 20. Tallahassee, FL: Tall Timbers Research Station: 374–379.

Annotation: See annotation in section II.C.2, page 22.

Brown, James K. 1992–1993. A case for management ignitions in wilderness. Fire Management Notes. 53/54(4): 3–8.

Annotation: Brown argues that prescribed fire is an important tool for maintaining natural conditions and wilderness character. In many wilderness areas, and particularly in those that are small, natural fire alone is insufficient or impractical to restore fire effects. For such areas, prescribed fire can supplement or act as a surrogate for natural fires. Prescribed fire can reduce fuel accumulations, reintroduce fire to areas no longer subject to natural fires, help balance the goals of fire restoration with other constraints such as endangered species protection, and allow burning at times when air quality regulations can be met. Brown suggests that prescribed fire programs be based on an understanding of fire's historical role in ecosystems, and he describes methods for gathering fire history data and comparing historical to current fire patterns. Though our understanding of fire as a natural disturbance and our ability to control prescribed fire are incomplete, we nonetheless must act, lest we face greater risks and losses in the long run.

Haase, Sally M.; Sackett, Stephen S. 1998. Effects of prescribed fire in giant sequoia-mixed conifer stands in Sequoia and Kings Canyon National Parks. In: Pruden, Teresa L.; Brennan, Leonard A., eds. Fire in ecosystem management: shifting the paradigm from suppression to prescription; 1996 May 7–10; Boise, ID. Tall Timbers Fire Ecology Conference Proceedings, No. 20. Tallahassee, FL: Tall Timbers Research Station: 236–243.

Annotation: See annotation in section I.B.2, page 8.

Hardy, Colin C.; Arno, Stephen F., eds. 1996. Proceedings: the use of fire in forest restoration: a general session at the annual meeting of the Society for Ecological Restoration; 1995 September 14–16; Seattle, WA. Ogden, UT: U.S. Department of Agriculture, Forest Service, Intermountain Research Station. 86 p.

Annotation: See annotation in section I.A, page 6.

Johnson, E. A.; Miyanishi, K. 1995. The need for consideration of fire behavior and effects in prescribed burning. Restoration Ecology. 3(4): 271–278.

Annotation: See annotation in section I.B.2, page 8.

Keeley, Jon E.; Stephenson, Nathan L. 2000. Restoring natural fire regimes to the Sierra Nevada in an era of global change. In: Cole, David N.; McCool, Stephen F.; Borrie, William T.; O'Loughlin, Jennifer, comps. Wilderness science in a time of change conference—Volume 5: wilderness ecosystems, threats, and management; 1999 May 23–27; Missoula, MT. Proc. RMRS-P-15-VOL-5. Ogden, UT: U.S. Department of Agriculture, Forest Service, Rocky Mountain Research Station: 266–269.

Annotation: This article outlines a framework for managing fire in protected areas based on the goal of restoring and maintaining natural ecosystems. The framework involves a step-by-step process, where managers and scientists model a "natural ecosystem" for a site, compare current ecosystems to this ideal, then plan, execute, and evaluate restoration aimed at achieving natural conditions. The paper also places fire restoration in the context of global changes in climate and land use patterns. Finally, Keeley and Stephenson identify research needed to refine and improve fire restoration in parks and wilderness. The paper deals with many current controversies in wilderness fire management, portraying the complexities generated by our limited ecological understanding of fire as well as philosophical and political issues in fire restoration.

Mangan, Richard J. 1985. Fire suppression for wilderness and parks: planning considerations. In: Lotan, James E.; Kilgore, Bruce M.; Fischer, William C.; Mutch, Robert W., eds. Proceedings—symposium and workshop on wilderness fire; 1983 November 15–18; Missoula, MT. Gen. Tech. Rep. INT-182. Ogden, UT: U.S. Department of Ag-

riculture, Forest Service, Intermountain Forest and Range Experiment Station: 159–161.

Annotation: Even as managers of parks and wilderness areas work to restore natural fire regimes, fire suppression will remain a part of wilderness management, and we should plan accordingly. Fire suppression techniques used in nonwilderness areas may be inappropriate in wilderness, and advance planning and prioritization is needed to minimize physical, visual, and audial impacts of suppression. Mangan emphasizes the need for fire suppression plans that consider the legal mandate to protect natural conditions and minimize human impacts as well as the unique characteristics of wilderness (for example, roadlessness).

Mohr, Francis. 1994. Fire suppression commensurate with wilderness stewardship. In: Sydoriak, Charisse, ed. 1994. Sixth national wilderness conference handbook: the spirit lives; 1994 November 14–18; Santa Fe, NM. Los Alamos, NM: U.S. Bureau of Land Management: 149–152.

Annotation: This brief article discusses the need to minimize impacts associated with fire suppression in wilderness. Mohr focuses on firelines, tree cutting, and helispot construction as activities that can be used sparingly or carried out in a minimal impact manner. After fire, rehabilitation can mitigate the impacts of suppression. To ensure effective control of fire suppression impacts, agency administrators must ensure that these impacts are considered during the planning process.

Mutch, Robert W. 1995. Prescribed fires in wilderness: how successful? In: Brown, James K.; Mutch, Robert, W.; Spoon, Charles W.; Wakimoto, Ronald H., tech. coords. Proceedings: symposium on fire in wilderness and park management. 1993 March 30–April 1; Missoula, MT. Gen. Tech. Rep. INT-GTR 320. Ogden, UT: U.S. Department of Agriculture, Forest Service, Intermountain Research Station: 38–41.

Annotation: Mutch asserts that the "perpetuation of natural ecosystems" is the objective of wilderness fire management, and that continued fire suppression cannot achieve this goal. Although naturally ignited and naturally burning fires are the ideal for wilderness, because they minimize human control, wilderness size, shape, and other considerations frequently preclude this option. Management-ignited prescribed fires therefore can be critical to restoration of wilderness fire. After providing this conceptual groundwork, Mutch outlines key considerations in wilderness fire management—including fire history, fire regimes, and fire effects—that set the context for planning. The paper next discusses criteria (often unmet in small wildernesses) that allow reliance on natural ignitions to perpetuate fire. Finally, the author outlines an eight-step process for developing fire management plans for small wilderness areas, recommending consideration of both prescribed natural fire and manager-ignited prescribed fire.

National Park Service; USDA Forest Service; Bureau of Indian Affairs; U.S. Fish and Wildlife Service; Bureau of Land Management. 1998. Wildland and prescribed fire management policy: implementation procedures and reference guide. Boise, ID: National Interagency Fire Center. 81 p. For additional information, contact: G. Thomas Zimmerman, tom_Zimmerman@nps.gov.

Annotation: See annotation in section II.F.1, page 29.

Nickas, George. 1998–1999. Wilderness fire. Wilderness Watcher. 10(1): 1, 4–5.

Annotation: In this paper, Nickas discusses wilderness fire policy and asserts that manipulation of fire in wilderness contradicts the spirit of the Wilderness Act. Both fire suppression and management-ignited prescribed fire diminish wilderness character and impede natural processes. Nickas outlines eight points that would support a natural role for wilderness fire. For example, development of wilderness fire plans on a landscape level, avoidance of fire breaks in wilderness, and minimal impact fire suppression all play an important role in managing a fire in a way that respects wilderness character.

Parsons, David J. 1998–1999. The dilemma of wilderness fire. Wilderness Watcher. 10(1): 12–13.

Annotation: See annotation in section II.F.1, page 30.

Pyne, Stephen J. 2001. The perils of prescribed fire: a reconsideration. Natural Resources Journal. 41: 1–8.

Annotation: In this paper, Pyne discusses problems with prescribed burning programs on Federal lands. Many prescribed burns have escaped, and some have even cost firefighters their lives. Additionally, prescribed burns haven't achieved management objectives, because they often burn too hot, cold, large or small. Pyne argues that we lack a good justification for prescribed fire. We need a justification that acknowledges both the ecological and human dimensions of fire, and we need improved practices for managing fire.

Pyne, Stephen, J.; Andrews, Patricia L.; Laven, Richard D. 1996a. Introduction to wildland fire—second edition. NY: John Wiley and Sons. 769 p.

Annotation: See annotation in section I.A, page 6.

Strohmaier, David J. 2000. The ethics of prescribed fire: a notable silence. Ecological Restoration. 18(1): 5–9.

Annotation: This brief paper asserts that ethical concerns are not adequately considered in planning prescribed fires. The primary goal of many prescribed fires—to restore ecosystem structure and function—exemplifies a valuing of "ecological wholes," and is ethically justified. However, Strohmaier raises the concern that ecological wholes are not the only ethical concern associated with prescribed fire, and that harm to individuals can result from an overemphasis on wholes. The author points out that prescribed burn plans generally consider animal mortality as nominal from a population perspective and take few measures to minimize harm to individual animals. If the lives of individual animals were better taken into account during the planning process, it might be possible to reduce, if not eliminate, harm to individuals caused by prescribed fire. The emphasis on wholes such as populations, species, and ecological processes should be tempered by consideration of individuals.

Tomascak, Walt. 1991. Improving a prescribed natural fire program: the Northern Region's approach. Fire Management Notes. 52(4): 6–8.

Annotation: This brief paper discusses revisions to Forest Service management practices for prescribed natural fire following the intense fires of 1988. Instead of requiring fire management decisions to occur rapidly with little documentation and contingency planning, the revised approach initiated a two-stage process involving an initial assessment and a detailed burn plan. Required components of a burn plan included an analysis of fire growth potential in light of weather projections, an assessment of the social and environmental impacts of the fire, and designation of a Maximum Allowable Perimeter for the fire. After outlining the new planning structure, Tomascak discusses the revised program's funding mechanisms and describes the challenges that emerged 2 years after implementation. Although wildland fire management has undergone further changes since this paper was written, the challenges and lessons Tomascak discusses may offer perspective on the evolution of fire management and insight into issues that persist today.

Whelan, Robert J. 1995b. Fire and management. In: Whelan, Robert J. The ecology of fire. NY: Cambridge University Press: 294–308.

Annotation: See annotation in section I.A, page 6.

2. Monitoring and Evaluating Fire Restoration

Boucher, Paul F.; Moody, Ronald D. 1998. The historical role of fire and ecosystem management of fires: Gila National Forest, New Mexico. In: Pruden, Teresa L.; Brennan, Leonard A., eds. Fire in ecosystem management: shifting the paradigm from suppression to prescription; 1996 May 7–10; Boise, ID. Tall Timbers Fire Ecology Conference Proceedings, No. 20. Tallahassee, FL: Tall Timbers Research Station: 374–379.

Annotation: This paper discusses the history and evolution of fire management on the New Mexico's Gila National Forest, where the Forest Service developed one of its first prescribed natural fire (PNF) programs. The authors describe the PNF program as an effort to reverse landscape changes that resulted from fire suppression and livestock grazing. Wilderness areas, which make up more than 20 percent of the Forest, served as an important source of baseline information in developing fire management plans, because these areas suffered fewer changes from fire suppression due to their remoteness. Boucher and Moody outline the agency's experience in restoring fire to the Gila, emphasizing the importance of public education, understanding and support. The roles of environmental laws, public response to smoke, and the fire classification system (wildfire versus PNF) are also discussed, and the program as a whole is evaluated.

Bradley, Anne F.; Arno, Stephen F. 1991. Using a fire regime classification to evaluate the effectiveness of the fire management program in the Selway-Bitterroot

Wilderness. In: Andrews, Patricia L.; Potts, Donald F., eds. Proceedings of the eleventh conference on fire and forest meteorology. Bethesda, MD: Society of American Foresters: 308–312.

Annotation: This brief paper describes a method for evaluating the success of a natural fire program in the Selway-Bitterroot Wilderness. Bradley and Arno describe a program evaluation technique that compares fire regimes since program implementation to pre-1935 fire regimes, which were unaffected by fire suppression. The approach uses aerial photographs and managers' recollections of past fires to reconstruct burned acreage and fire severity. Because complete and accurate information is hard to obtain using these methods, the authors recommend better documentation of prescribed natural fires and include a sample form for keeping fire records.

Brown, James K.; Arno, Stephen F.; Barrett, Stephen W.; Menakis, James P. 1994. Comparing the prescribed natural fire program with presettlement fires in the Selway-Bitterroot Wilderness. International Journal of Wildland Fire. 4(3): 157–168.

Annotation: See annotation in section I.C.2, page 11.

Caprio, Anthony C.; Graber, David M. 2000. Returning fire to the mountains: can we successfully restore the ecological role of pre-European fire regimes to the Sierra Nevada? In: Cole, David N.; McCool, Stephen F.; Borrie, William T.; O'Loughlin, Jennifer, comps. Proceedings: Wilderness science in a time of change—Volume 5: wilderness ecosystems, threats, and management; 1999 May 23–27; Missoula, MT. Proc. RMRS-P-15-VOL-5. Ogden, UT: U.S. Department of Agriculture, Forest Service, Rocky Mountain Research Station: 233–241.

Annotation: In this study, Caprio and Graber used two techniques to evaluate fire management in Sequoia and King's Canyon National Parks. First, they reconstructed annual burn area for the pre-European settlement era using mean and maximum fire return intervals from tree ring analyses dating back to 1700. These estimated burn areas then were compared to areas burned during the 20th century. Second, Caprio and Graber calculated the Fire Return Interval Departure for different vegetation types, comparing the time since last fire to the maximum average fire return interval calculated from historical records. Results were used to compare fire patterns during the presettlement era, under fire suppression, and since reintroduction of fire in the late 1960s. The article discusses strengths and weaknesses of the two evaluation methods and identifies areas for additional research. Finally, the authors discuss social, political, logistical, and epistemological factors that constrain restoration of fire as a natural process.

Keifer, MaryBeth; Stephenson, Nathan L.; Manley, Jeff. 2000. Prescribed fire as the minimum tool for wilderness forest and fire regime restoration: a case study from the Sierra Nevada, California. In: Cole, David N.; McCool, Stephen F.; Borrie, William T.; O'Loughlin, Jennifer, comps. Wilderness science in a time of change conference—Volume 5: wilderness ecosystems, threats, and management; 1999 May 23–27; Missoula, MT. Proc.

RMRS-P-15-VOL-5. Ogden, UT: U.S. Department of Agriculture, Forest Service, Rocky Mountain Research Station: 266–269.

Annotation: In this short paper, Keifer and others describe monitoring following prescribed burning for fire and forest restoration in Sequoia and Kings Canyon National Parks. Using multiple historical data sources, targets for forest stand structure were developed for the parks. The authors then compared stand densities before and after prescribed burns to these targets, in order to evaluate the effectiveness of the fire management program in restoring pre-European settlement conditions. The utility of this simple monitoring approach is discussed, as are additional indicators such as recruitment of key tree species.

Miller, Carol; Urban, Dean L. 2000. Modeling the effects of fire management alternatives on Sierra Nevada mixed-conifer forests. Ecological Applications. 10(1): 85–94.

Annotation: The authors used a simulation model to investigate three strategies for restoring fire to forests in the Sierra Nevada: harvest, prescribed fire, and natural fire. All three treatments were effective in restoring pre-suppression basal area and forest composition. However, prescribed fire and natural fire acted more slowly than harvest. The paper may be useful to managers interested in modeling alternative fire treatments for wildland restoration. Limitations of this model, and models generally, are also discussed. Changes in ignition frequency and fire spread due to increased grazing and cessation of Native American burning, for example, may be important factors influencing fire patterns and forest structure today. However, these variables were not included in the model.

Parsons, David J. 1990. Restoring fire to the Sierra Nevada mixed conifer forest: reconciling science, policy, and practicality. In: Hughes, H. G.; Bonnicksen, T. M., eds. Proceedings of the first annual meeting of the Society for Ecological Restoration; [Date of conference unknown]; Madison, WI. University of Wisconsin, Madison: 271–279.

Annotation: This paper discusses fire restoration in mixed conifer forests of Sequoia and Kings Canyon National Parks, with a focus on defining goals and evaluating program success. Goals for fire management in Sequoia and Kings Canyon embrace the broader Park Service goal of maintaining natural ecosystems, though striving toward "naturalness" is both conceptually ambiguous and technically challenging. Managers, however, must inevitably act with incomplete knowledge, balancing multiple factors such as policy, cost, and practicality. In restoring fire to the Sierra Nevada, ecological process goals were favored over restoring forest structure. Within the broad goal of restoring ecological processes, specific techniques have changed over time. When prescribed burning began in the late 1960s, uniform, high-intensity fires were the norm. More recently, prescribed burning has shifted to patchier, mixed-intensity fires. To refine and improve goals and techniques over time, additional fire research is needed and criteria for evaluating success are key.

Parsons, David J.; Botti, Stephen J. 1996. Restoration of fire in National Parks. In: Hardy, Colin C.; Arno,

Stephen F., eds. The use of fire in forest restoration. Gen. Tech. Rep. INT-GTR-341. Ogden, UT: U.S. Department of Agriculture, Forest Service, Intermountain Research Station: 29–31.

Annotation: See annotation in section II.A, page 18.

Parsons, David J.; Landres, Peter B. 1998. Restoring natural fire to wilderness: how are we doing? In: Pruden, Teresa L.; Brennan, Leonard A., eds. Fire in ecosystem management: shifting the paradigm from suppression to prescription; 1996 May 7–10; Boise, ID. Tall Timbers Fire Ecology Conference Proceedings No. 20. Tallahassee, FL: Tall Timbers Research Station: 366–373.

Annotation: See annotation in section II.A, page 18.

Saveland, James M. 1986. Wilderness fire economics: the Frank Church-River of No Return Wilderness. In: Lucas, R. C., ed. Proceedings: national wilderness research conference: issues, state-of-knowledge, future directions; 1985 July 23–26; Fort Collins, CO. Gen. Tech. Rep. INT-220. Ogden, UT: U.S. Department of Agriculture, Forest Service, Intermountain Research Station: 39–48.

Annotation: See annotation in section II.D.3, page 27.

Stephenson, Nathan L. 1999. Reference conditions for giant sequoia restoration: structure, process, and precision. Ecological Applications. 9(4): 1253–1265.

Annotation: Knowledge of reference conditions has played a key in fire restoration to the Sierra Nevada National Parks. However even in the well-studied sequoia forest ecosystem, we lack complete knowledge about past forest structure. Understanding of past fire regimes is somewhat better, though still imperfect. Uncertainty about past conditions and the interactions between forest structure and disturbance processes has sparked debate over fire restoration methods, with some scientists ("process restorationists") recommending that reintroducing fire is sufficient to restore natural processes and conditions while others ("structural restorationists") assert that mechanical thinning should precede fire restoration. The author argues that mechanical techniques may not be necessary to restore the Sierra Nevada sequoia groves. However, a number of caveats are discussed, including the fact that process-based restoration may not be sufficient to restore all forest ecosystems.

Taylor, A. H. 2000. Fire regimes and forest changes in mid and upper montane forests of southern Cascades, Lassen Volcanic Park, California, U.S.A. Journal of Biogeography. 27: 87–104.

Annotation: See annotation in section I.C.2, page 12.

van Wagtendonk, Jan W. 1996. Use of a deterministic fire growth model test fuel treatments. In: Sierra Nevada Ecosystem Project: Final report to Congress, Vol. II, Assessments and scientific basis for management options. Davis: University of California, Centers for Water and Wildland Resources: 1155–1165.

Annotation: This paper reports on the effectiveness of different strategies for reducing fuels in areas affected by fire suppression. Using simulation models, van Wagtendonk investigated the effects of different types of fuels treatments on fire spread and intensity. Prescribed burning was most effective in reducing rate of spread, fireline intensity, flame length, and heat per unit area, whereas overstory thinning increased spread rate, flame length and intensity relative to the control. The effects of understory fuel removal depended on the nature of the treatment (cut-and-scatter versus pile-and-burn). The author also examined fuel break effectiveness, finding that fuel breaks are insufficient to control fires in the absence of other fuel treatments. This study used the model FARSITE, with a number of simplifying assumptions. Improved site-specific information, particularly spatially accurate fuels data, would improve modeling accuracy and better predict the consequences of different management strategies.

D. Considerations and Constraints on Restoring Wilderness Fire

Although many ecologists and land managers recognize fire's pivotal role in maintaining natural ecological processes, wilderness fire restoration remains contentious, and managers must consider numerous factors in restoration planning. The papers in this section highlight a number of the legal, social, political, and economic issues associated with wilderness fire management. In the legal realm, the Wilderness Act, the Clean Water Act, the Clean Air Act, the Endangered Species Act, and the National Historic Preservation Act all shape fire planning. The social perception of fire and its associated risks, as well as the costs of different fire management strategies, also should be taken into account.

1. Legal

Bryan, Dana C., ed. 1997. Conference proceedings: environmental regulation and prescribed fire: legal and social challenges; Tampa Airport Hilton at MetroCenter, Tampa, FL; 1995 March 14–17; Tallahassee, FL: Center for Professional Development, Florida State University. 246 p. Available: Division of Forestry, Florida Department of Agriculture and Consumer Services, 3125 Conner Boulevard, Tallahassee, FL 32399-1650.

Annotation: This proceedings examines the legal and social constraints on prescribed fire. Papers include assessments of numerous key environmental laws—the Clean Air Act, Clean Water Act, Wilderness Act, Endangered Species Act, and others—in relation to management-ignited fire. In addition, a number of authors discuss legal liability for damage associated with prescribed fire and the implications of liability for planning and management. Finally, social aspects of prescribed fire (for example, public acceptability) are addressed. A number of papers contained in the proceedings are annotated below.

Bunnell, David L. 1997. Prescribed fire consideration and the Wilderness Act. In: Bryan, Dana C., ed. Conference proceedings: environmental regulation and prescribed fire: legal and social challenges; 1995 March 14-17; Tampa Airport Hilton at MetroCenter, Tampa, FL. Tallahassee,

FL: Florida State University, Center for Professional Development: 64–73.

Annotation: In this paper, Bunnell discusses the contested implications of the Wilderness Act for fire management, discussing ambiguities in the language of the law. Additionally, numerous constraints on prescribed fire in wilderness are discussed, including those stemming from environmental laws and from risks to recreational opportunities, structures, and endangered species. Bunnell provides an example from the Bob Marshall Wilderness, showing how negotiation of prescribed natural fire boundaries must take multiple factors (for example, recreation, cultural resources) into account. The author concludes that wilderness fire management requires a holistic approach where many considerations, including long-term effects, play a role in decisionmaking.

Core, John E. 1997. Air quality regulations: treatment of emissions from wildfires vs. prescribed fires. In: Bryan, D. C., ed. Conference proceedings: environmental regulation and prescribed fire: legal and social challenges; 1995 March 14–17; Tampa Airport Hilton at MetroCenter, Tampa, FL. Tallahassee, FL: Florida State University, Center for Professional Development: 53–62.

Annotation: Restoration of wilderness fire relies on wildland fire and management-ignited prescribed fire, both of which emit particulate and gaseous air pollutants regulated by the Clean Air Act. This paper discusses fire-generated emissions in the context of air quality regulations and control measures. Core identifies key issues surrounding smoke policies, including the classification of fire-generated pollution as anthropogenic versus natural, and the integration of wildland fire emissions into state-level air planning.

Knopp, Christopher M. 1995. Impacts of the Clean Water Act on prescribed fire in the western United States. In: Bryan, D. C., ed. Conference proceedings: environmental regulation and prescribed fire: legal and social challenges; 1995 March 14–17; Tampa Airport Hilton at MetroCenter, Tampa, FL. Tallahassee, FL: Florida State University, Center for Professional Development: 100–104.

Annotation: This short paper briefly explains the structure of the Clean Water Act (CWA) and its relevance to prescribed fire. Prescribed fire falls under the CWA due to increased erosion that can occur in burned areas where less live vegetation exists to protect the soil. Because erosion is a spatially diffuse process, it is regulated under the nonpoint source provisions of the CWA. The paper discusses nonpoint source control regulations for waters under different levels of protection and emphasizes the necessity of designating and monitoring Best Management Practices to control the effects of fire on water quality.

Knudsen, Gary D. 1995. Overview of cultural resources act requirements (overview of heritage resources and prescribed fire). In: Bryan, D. C., ed. Conference proceedings: environmental regulation and prescribed fire: legal and social challenges; 1995 March 14–17; Tampa Airport Hilton at MetroCenter, Tampa, FL. Tallahassee, FL: Florida State University, Center for Professional Development: 105–112.

Annotation: Many protected areas, particularly National Parks and monuments, contain archaeological or historic management activities. This paper explains how heritage resource management can be compatible with prescribed fire and discusses both the potential positive and negative effects of prescribed fire on historic resources. In addition, the author outlines the planning process under the National Historic Preservation Act and suggests that careful fire planning can benefit both ecological and cultural resources.

LaRosa, Anne Marie; Floyd, M. Lisa. 1995. Predicting fire effects on rare plant taxa: a management perspective. In: Brown, James K.; Mutch, Robert W.; Spoon, Charles W.; Wakimoto, Ronald H., tech. coords. 1995. Proceedings: symposium on fire in wilderness and park management; 1993 March 30–April 1; Missoula, MT. Gen. Tech. Rep. INT-GTR-320. Ogden, UT: U.S. Department of Agriculture, Forest Service, Intermountain Research Station: 83–88.

Annotation: This paper discusses the relationship between rare plant protection and fire management in protected areas. The Endangered Species Act obligates Federal agencies to protect threatened and endangered species. However, in some cases this mandate may conflict with wilderness management goals such as fire restoration. The authors suggest that risk analyses for sensitive plant species can assist in balancing the goals of fire management and biodiversity protection. LaRosa and Floyd identify data and information needs for such analyses, then provide two examples (from Colorado's Mesa Verde National Park and Arizona's Buenos Aires National Wildlife Refuge) to show how ecological information can help clarify risks and improve fire risk management for endangered species.

Procter, Trent. 1995. Working to make the Clean Air Act and prescribed burning compatible. In: Weise, David R.; Martin, Robert E., tech. coords. The Biswell symposium: fire issues and solutions in urban interface and wildland ecosystems; 1994 February 15–17; Walnut Creek, CA. Gen. Tech. Rep. PSW-GTR-158. Albany, CA: U.S. Department of Agriculture, Forest Service, Pacific Southwest Research Station: 125–128.

Annotation: This short paper outlines the history of the Clean Air Act of 1963 and describes the relationship between the 1990 amendments to the act and prescribed fire. The authors identify four categories relevant to prescribed fire management: particulate matter (PM10) standards, conformity with state-level plans, air toxics, and visibility. Additionally, the paper points out six solutions to conflicts between air quality and the use of fire to maintain ecosystem health. These solutions primarily focus on communication and coordinated planning. Although written with a focus on California, the paper contains background and recommendations that should be relevant to fire managers nationwide.

White, David H. 1991. Legal implications associated with use and control of fire as a management practice. In: High intensity fire in wildlands: management challenges and options; 1989 May 18–21; Tallahassee, FL. Tall Timbers Fire Conference Proceedings No. 17. Tallahassee, FL: Tall Timbers Research Station: 375–384.

Annotation: This paper offers a brief overview of legal issues associated with fire management, with an emphasis on liability. Legal liability for fire today generally requires negligence to be proved. However, some states have instituted safety laws that reverse the burden of proof. In this case, the defendant must show that "due care" was exercised to avoid liability. In the latter part of the paper, the author discusses the potential for a positive obligation to use management-ignited fires to reduce fire hazard or protect endangered species. This article contains information relevant to the management of fire at wilderness boundaries.

2. Social and Political

Beebe, Grant S.; Omi, Philip N. 1993. Wildland burning: the perception of risk. Journal of Forestry. 91(9): 19–24.

Annotation: See annotation in section II.E, page 28.

Bright, Alan D. 1995. Influencing public attitudes toward prescribed fire policies. In: Bryan, D. C., ed. Conference proceedings: environmental regulation and prescribed fire: legal and social challenges; 1995 March 14–17; Tampa Airport Hilton at MetroCenter, Tampa, FL. Tallahassee, FL: Florida State University, Center for Professional Development: 147–154.

Annotation: In the years following the 1988 fires in Yellowstone National Park, a number of studies examined changes in public attitudes toward prescribed fire. Few differences were found between surveys immediately after the fire and those conducted 5 to 6 years later. Bright suggests that greater shifts in public opinion might be realized through persuasive communication by land managers. A variety of factors influence the effectiveness of communication, including audience understanding, repetition, relevance, and prior knowledge. Bright discusses these and other factors, providing specific recommendations to managers seeking to influence public sentiment about prescribed fire.

Brown, James K.; Bradshaw, Larry S. 1994. Comparisons of particulate emissions and smoke impacts from presettlement, full suppression, and prescribed natural fire periods in the Selway-Bitterroot Wilderness. International Journal of Wildland Fire. 4(3): 143–155.

Annotation: This study compares smoke and particulate emissions from the Selway-Bitterrroot Wilderness under different fire management regimes. Using historical and ecological data, the authors estimated fire area, particulate emissions, and valley smoke events in both presettlement and recent times. Area burned annually was greater during the presettlement period than in recent decades, and particulate emissions were slightly higher. The study results suggest that fires generated more smoke during the presettlement era than in recent times. However, recent fires produced a greater amount of smoke per hectare. The implications of these findings for wilderness fire management are briefly discussed.

Bunnell, David L. 1997. Prescribed fire consideration and the Wilderness Act. In: Bryan, D. C., ed. Conference proceedings: environmental regulation and prescribed fire: legal and social challenges; 1995 March 14–17; Tampa Airport Hilton at MetroCenter, Tampa, FL. Tallahassee,

FL: Florida State University, Center for Professional Development: 64–73.

Annotation: See annotation in section II.D.1, page 24.

Caprio, Anthony C.; Graber, David M. 2000. Returning fire to the mountains: can we successfully restore the ecological role of pre-European fire regimes to the Sierra Nevada? In: Cole, David N.; McCool, Stephen F.; Borrie, William T.; O'Loughlin, Jennifer, comps. Proceedings: Wilderness science in a time of change—Volume 5: wilderness ecosystems, threats, and management; 1999 May 23–27; Missoula, MT. Proc. RMRS-P-15-VOL-5. Ogden, UT: U.S. Department of Agriculture, Forest Service, Rocky Mountain Research Station: 233–241.

Annotation: See annotation in section II.C.2, page 23.

Manfredo, Michael J.; Fishbein, Martin; Haas, Glenn E.; Watson, Alan E. 1990. Attitudes toward prescribed fire policies. Journal of Forestry. 88(7): 19–23.

Annotation: This study examined public attitudes and beliefs about "controlled burn" fire policies in the wake of the 1988 fires in Yellowstone National Park. Manfredo and others surveyed citizens from across the United States, and analyzed survey results on national (all states but Montana and Wyoming) and regional (Montana and Wyoming) scales. The regional population slightly favored controlled burning, while the national population split on the issue. Attitudes toward controlled burning correlated with beliefs about the consequences of prescribed burning, and those who favored controlled burning tended to be better informed about its ecological effects. The implications of these results for management and public education are discussed.

McCool, Stephen F.; Stankey, George H. 1986. Visitor attitudes toward wilderness fire management policy—1971–84. Res. Pap. INT-357. Ogden, UT: U.S. Department of Agriculture, Forest Service, Rocky Mountain Research Station. 7 p.

Annotation: In this study, the authors surveyed wilderness visitors' knowledge of and attitudes toward fire and compared survey results to the results of a similar survey 13 years earlier (in 1971). Knowledge of fire effects was greater in 1984 than in 1971, and participants in the later survey held more favorable views toward natural fire management than their earlier counterparts, the majority of whom favored fire suppression. The paper also explores justifications for survey respondents' attitudes toward fire and discusses the relationship between knowledge, attitudes, and public education.

Plevel, Steve R. 1997. Fire policy at the wildland-urban interface. Journal of Forestry. 95(10): 12–17.

Annotation: Based on a literature review and three case studies, Plevel discusses policymaking for fire at the wildland-urban interface. Although the author asserts that policymaking responsibility lies largely with local governments, he also points out that wildland fires often cross administrative boundaries and require involvement of multiple institutions. The article offers insight into the urban side of wildland fire management and may help Federal agencies identify opportunities to coordinate with local governments in managing the risks posed by wilderness fire.

Procter, Trent. 1995. Working to make the Clean Air Act and prescribed burning compatible. In: Weise, David R.; Martin, Robert E., tech. coords. The Biswell symposium: fire issues and solutions in urban interface and wildland ecosystems; 1994 February 15–17; Walnut Creek, CA. Gen. Tech. Rep. PSW-GTR-158. Albany, CA: U.S. Department of Agriculture, Forest Service, Pacific Southwest Research Station: 125–128.

Annotation: See annotation in section II.D.1, page 25.

Smith, Conrad. 1991. Yellowstone media myths: print and television coverage of the 1988 fires. In: Nodvin, Stephen C.; Waldrop, Thomas A., eds. Fire and the environment: ecological and cultural perspectives: proceedings of an international symposium; 1990 March 20–24; Knoxville, TN. Gen. Tech. Rep. SE-69. Asheville, NC: U.S. Department of Agriculture, Forest Service, Southeastern Forest Experiment Station: 321–327.

Annotation: Smith examines the media coverage surrounding the famed "fires of '88" in Yellowstone National Park. The stories in national and local newspapers, as well as on national television networks, were analyzed and compared, showing that coverage differed among sources and locations. Factual errors were not uncommon in reporting on the fires, and some of these inaccuracies reinforced existing myths about fire management and fire effects. Much of the confusion in the press surrounded the Park Service's natural fire policy and its role in the Yellowstone fires. The study illustrates the challenges fire managers may face in communicating with media and consequently, in providing accurate information to the public.

Taylor, Jonathan G.; Mutch, Robert W. 1986. Fire in wilderness: public knowledge, acceptance, and perceptions. In: Lucas, R. C., ed. Proceedings: national wilderness research conference: issues, state-of-knowledge, future directions; 1985 July 23–26; Fort Collins, CO. Gen. Tech. Rep. INT-220. Ogden, UT: U.S. Department of Agriculture, Forest Service, Intermountain Research Station: 49–59.

Annotation: This article reviews a number of studies on public knowledge and perceptions of wilderness fire. Surveys show that public acceptance of fire tends to increase with knowledge, particularly of the beneficial effects of fire. Additionally, public information and education materials can be effective in changing people's understanding of and attitudes toward fire. Taylor and Mutch point out that public awareness of fire's beneficial effects appears to have increased, but in some areas (for example, animal mortality), public knowledge is limited or inaccurate. The authors stress that an individual's general attitudes toward fire (in principle) may not match with his/her personal reaction to fire (in practice), and that managers need to be aware of this disjunction. Additionally, education should be bi-directional, with managers informing the public but also learning from the public through surveys and other assessments.

3. Economic

Botti, Stephen J. 1999. The National Park Service wildland fire management program. In: Gonzalez-Caban, Armando; Omi, Philip N., tech. coords. Proceedings of the symposium on fire economics, planning, and policy: bottom lines; 1999 April 5–9; San Diego, CA. Gen. Tech. Rep. PSW-GTR-173. Albany, CA: U.S. Department of Agriculture, Forest Service, Pacific Southwest Research Station: 7–14.

Annotation: This paper provides an overview of the National Park Service fire management program and its economics. Botti emphasizes the need to evaluate the cost effectiveness of Park Service fire programs with respect to the parks' fire management goals. These goals emphasize restoring and maintaining the natural role of fire while protecting against unwanted wildland fires that endanger lives, structures, or other resources such as critical habitat for endangered species. Because of their unique values, parks and protected areas demand different types of economic analyses than commodity-production lands. Botti identifies the three areas of fire management expenditures in the Park Service—readiness and program management, fuels management and prescribed fire, and wildland fire response—and describes the Park Service's approach to evaluating fire program effectiveness.

Childers, Christian A.; Piirto, Douglas D. 1991. Cost-effective wilderness fire management: a case study in southern California. In: Nodvin, Stephen C.; Waldrop, Thomas A., eds. 1991. Fire and the environment: ecological and cultural perspectives: proceedings of an international symposium; 1990 March 20–24; Knoxville, TN. Gen. Tech. Rep. SE-69. Asheville, NC: U.S. Department of Agriculture, Forest Service, Southeast Forest Experiment Station: 179–185.

Annotation: This paper uses an economic analysis to assess alternative strategies for managing fire in southern California's Dick Smith and San Rafael Wilderness Areas. Different fire management alternatives are evaluated based on their ability to promote a natural fire regime while minimizing costs. Results suggest that containment may be more effective than full suppression in achieving the desired objective. Problems in assigning economic values to wilderness are also discussed.

Saveland, James M. 1986. Wilderness fire economics: the Frank Church-River of No Return Wilderness. In: Lucas, R. C., ed. Proceedings: National wilderness research conference: issues, state-of-knowledge, future directions; 1985 July 23–26; Fort Collins, CO. Gen. Tech. Rep. INT-220. Ogden, UT: U.S. Department of Agriculture, Forest Service, Intermountain Research Station: 39–48.

Annotation: This article provides a comparative analysis of four fire management options for the Frank Church-River of No Return Wilderness (FCRNRW) in central Idaho. Both economic and resource costs and benefits of fire management are considered under alternatives ranging from full suppression to a strategy that incorporates both natural and human-ignited prescribed fires. In this paper, the wilderness resource costs and benefits are gauged by how closely the area burned under a particular management scheme matches the historical fire regime. Economic cost estimates are based on costs of fire suppression, fire monitoring, and administration of prescribed burns from the FCRNRW and other similar wilderness areas. After presenting the results of his analysis, the author places the results into a decisionmaking context that incorporates risk.

E. Managing Risk

Restoring fire to wilderness entails risks—to natural resources, public and private property, and even human life. The articles in this section discuss the perception and management of risks related to wildland fire. Both managers and the public deal with fire risk, but generally from different perspectives. Beebe and Omi (1993) and Gardner and others (1987) report on public perceptions of risk and describe management approaches in response to public concerns. Cortner and others (1990) examine Forest Service managers' perceptions of risk. Other papers address legal liabilities associated with fire (Stanton 1995; White 1991) and Geographic Information Systems approaches to modeling and visualizing fire-related risks at landscape scales (Miller and others 2000; Sampson and others 2000).

Beebe, Grant S.; Omi, Philip N. 1993. Wildland burning: the perception of risk. Journal of Forestry. 91(9): 19–24.

Annotation: The academic literature gives little attention to wildland fire as a natural hazard, according to the authors, who here apply risk and natural hazard research to fire management issues. This paper discusses the challenges faced by managers seeking both to allow fire as a natural process and to minimize harm to the public. Patterns in public risk perception and response—such as the tendency to wait for an event to occur rather than take preventative measures—are discussed. Public perceptions of risk can be shaped strongly by media coverage, which tends to highlight dramatic and spectacular risks rather than longer-term, but similarly dangerous threats. Communication with the public can play an important role in increasing awareness and facilitating democratic participation in decisionmaking about fire risks and their management.

Cortner, Hanna J.; Taylor, Jonathan G.; Carpenter, Edwin H.; Cleaves, David A. 1990. Factors influencing Forest Service fire managers' risk behavior. Forest Science. 36(3): 531–548.

Annotation: This study used a mail survey to investigate fire managers' responses to different types and levels of risk in a variety of fire scenarios. The survey separately considered decisions relating to escaped wildfires, prescribed burning, and long-range planning for fire budgets. Managers' responses were complex and varied from region to region and under different conditions. Safety and risk to timber and wildlife habitat ranked high among the factors that managers took into consideration. Official policy and the possibility of reprimand from a supervisor ranked much lower. The article concludes by discussing the survey's implications for changing managers' fire management behavior.

Gardner, Philip D.; Cortner, Hanna J.; Widaman, Keith. 1987. The risk perceptions and policy response toward wildland fire hazards by urban homeowners. Landscape and Urban Planning. 14: 163–172.

Annotation: In this study, the authors examined how homeowners' perceptions of fire risk related to policy preferences regarding fire. Gardner and others describe three general possibilities for reducing property losses to fire: (1) modifying landscape characteristics, (2) changing building design, and (3) minimizing the human exposure to fire (for example, via residential zoning). The responses of two southern California communities—one which recently experienced fire, and the other which was unaffected by fire—are discussed. High initial awareness of fire risk correlated with high later awareness, although some residents of fire-affected communities felt it unlikely that fire would return. Homeowners' preferences for "technological fixes" over measures such as zoning are discussed in light of their wildland management implications.

Miller, Carol; Landres, Peter B.; Alaback, Paul B. 2000. Evaluating risks and benefits of wildland fire at landscape scales. In: Neuenschwander, L. F.; Ryan, K. C., tech. eds. Proceedings of crossing the millennium: integrating spatial technologies and ecological principles for a new age in fire management; Moscow, ID: University of Idaho: 78–87.

Annotation: In this paper, Miller and others describe a GIS-based, landscape model for evaluating fire risks and benefits. The model uses the probability of fire occurrence, the expected fire severity, and the social and ecological values associated with fire to generate maps showing fire risks and benefits across the landscape. These maps can assist managers in selecting and prioritizing fire management strategies based on landscape characteristics and social values. For example, in an area where risks associated with fire are minimal and the benefits high, the use of wildland fire may be appropriate to restore natural processes. In the opposite situation, a different tool might be used to mitigate risks while retaining ecosystem integrity. The paper describes model outcomes for the Selway-Bitterroot Ecosystem of Idaho and Montana and explains how model results can be applied to management.

Sampson, R. Neil; Atkinson, R. Dwight; Lewis, Joe W. 2000. Mapping wildfire hazards and risks. [Co-published simultaneously as Journal of Sustainable Forestry, volume 11, numbers 1/2 2000.] New York: Food Products Press. 328 p.

Annotation: This volume reports the results of a scientific workshop on wildfire hazards and risks, and though the chapters focus on Colorado ecosystems, the approaches are broadly relevant. The book's chapters illustrate how Geographic Information Systems can be used to analyze fire risks from both social and biophysical perspectives. On the biophysical side, chapters consider the risks associated with severe and large-scale fires, postfire erosion and sedimentation, and changes in habitat for sensitive species. Additionally, social and economic risks are considered, and four chapters discuss the air quality risks and wildland fire. The editors suggest that this volume can assist in strategic planning for fire management and increase the efficiency of fire-related spatial analyses.

Stanton, Robert. 1995. Managing liability exposures associated with prescribed fires. Natural Areas Journal. 15: 347–352.

Annotation: This article discusses risk management for prescribed fire in light of legal liability under the tort law. Different types of liability and associated legal standards are discussed, with specific examples of lawsuits related to prescribed fire. Stanton identifies three major fire liability issues: escaped fires, smoke-related damage, and accidents involving fire personnel. In each area, the author outlines the potential risks and methods for managing these risks, asserting that risk management is ecologically preferable to risk aversion, where prescribed fires are avoided in order to prevent liability.

White, David H. 1991. Legal implications associated with use and control of fire as a management practice. In: High intensity fire in wildlands: management challenges and options; 1989 May 18–21; Tallahassee, FL. Tall Timbers Fire Conference Proceedings No. 17. Tallahassee, FL: Tall Timbers Research Station: 375–384.

Annotation: See annotation in section II.D.1, page 25.

F. Current Wilderness Fire Issues

The papers in this section touch on a number of current issues and controversies in wilderness fire management. Topics include fire policy, the challenges posed by fires burning across administrative boundaries, the implications of global climate change for fire management, and air quality issues associated with wildland fire. Because development at the wildland-urban interface increasingly affects fire management in wilderness, we have included a section on fire at the wildland-urban interface. Also covered is the issue of mechanical thinning to restore historic vegetation structure before reintroducing fire—a strategy that many believe stretches the bounds of acceptable manipulation in wilderness too far.

1. Policy and Management

Cole, David N. 1996. Ecological manipulation in wilderness—an emerging management dilemma. International Journal of Wilderness. 2(1): 15–19.

Annotation: Cole discusses three different management goals put forth in Wilderness Act: (1) to preserve lands in "natural condition"; (2) to protect lands from human manipulation; and (3) to provide public benefits. The author argues that wilderness management entails "[optimizing] trade-offs between these three goals." In the management of fire, conflicts arise between preserving lands (goal 1) and protecting them from human intervention (goal 2). Do we intervene (for example, utilize management-ignited fires) to preserve "naturalness"? Cole suggests that the best solution may be a compromise between two extremes, and argues that we need to differentiate acceptable from unac-

ceptable restorations in wilderness. Potential criteria for appropriate restoration are discussed.

Czech, Brian. 1996. Challenges to establishing and implementing sound natural fire policy. Renewable Resources Journal. 14(2): 14–19.

Annotation: Czech argues that we should abandon major fire suppression efforts and restore natural fire regimes, based on ecological, practical, and fiscal considerations. The article then places this argument in a policy context, outlining the history of fire management by the U.S. Forest Service, National Park Service, Bureau of Land Management, and U.S. Fish and Wildlife Service. Finally, 11 impediments to natural fire regimes are discussed, ranging from political barriers to risks to human health and property.

Kilgore, Bruce M. 1986. The role of fire in wilderness: a state-of-the-knowledge review. In: Lucas, R. C., ed. Proceedings: national wilderness research conference: issues, state-of-knowledge, future directions; 1985 July 23–26; Fort Collins, CO. Gen. Tech. Rep. INT-220. Ogden, UT: U.S. Department of Agriculture, Forest Service, Intermountain Research Station: 70–103.

Annotation: See annotation in section I.A, page 6.

National Park Service; USDA Forest Service; Bureau of Indian Affairs; U.S. Fish and Wildlife Service; Bureau of Land Management. 1998. Wildland and prescribed fire management policy: implementation procedures and reference guide. Boise, ID: National Interagency Fire Center. 81 p. For additional information, contact: G. Thomas Zimmerman, tom_Zimmerman@nps.gov.

Annotation: This guide outlines procedures for fire management under the 1995 Federal Wildland Fire Management Policy and Program Review. It describes changes in terminology associated with the 1995 policy and details the three stages of a Wildland Fire Implementation Plan (WFIP). Additionally, the guide explains the planning process for prescribed fire. An appendix provides blank forms for documenting the WFIP process and for assessing the wildland fire situation. Throughout the document, flowcharts, tables, and timelines assist in identifying key points for wildland fire management.

Parsons, David J. 2000. The challenge of restoring natural fire to wilderness. In: Cole, David N.; McCool, Stephen F.; Borrie, William T.; O'Loughlin, Jennifer, comps. Wilderness science in a time of change conference—Volume 5: wilderness ecosystems, threats, and management; 1999 May 23–27; Missoula, MT. Proc. RMRS-P-15-VOL-5. Ogden, UT: U.S. Department of Agriculture, Forest Service, Rocky Mountain Research Station: 276–282.

Annotation: This paper outlines the history of fire management in parks and wilderness from the early 20th century until the present. Fire suppression dominated until the late 1960s, when Sequoia and Kings Canyon National Parks and others began to reintroduce fire. However, the trend toward fire restoration reversed after the fires of 1988, in the wake of a national fire policy review. Parsons discusses the role of natural and management-ignited fires since 1988 and presents choices for wilderness fire management in the future.

Parsons, David J. 1998–1999. The dilemma of wilderness fire. Wilderness Watcher. 10(1): 12–13.

Annotation: This short article asserts that fire is crucial to wilderness preservation. However, fire suppression has dominated and continues to dominate wilderness fire management. After briefly outlining fire management in the National Park Service, Forest Service, Fish and Wildlife Service, and Bureau of Land Management, the author discusses the consequences of continued suppression and identifies various options for managing wilderness fire.

U.S. Department of the Interior; U.S. Department of Agriculture; Department of Energy; Department of Defense; Department of Commerce; U.S. Environmental Protection Agency; Federal Emergency Management Agency; National Association of State Foresters. 2001. Review and update of the 1995 Federal Wildland Fire Management Policy. Boise, ID: National Interagency Fire Center. Available: National Interagency Fire Center, Attn: External Affairs Office, 3833 South Development Avenue, Boise, ID 83705-5354, (208) 387-5457 and http://www.nifc.gov/fire_policy/index.html. 78 p.

Annotation: This document replaces the 1995 Federal Wildland Fire Policy and provides the foundation for fire management on Federal public lands. The Review and Update generally affirms the 1995 policy, but identifies a few deficiencies in the original plan as well as problems with its implementation. The policy recommends better integration of fire management with existing land management plans, greater coordination among agencies with fire management responsibilities, increased attention to fire hazards at the wildland-urban interface, and better communication with the public about the natural role of fire. The document aims to provide a shared philosophical and political foundation for wildland fire management across the United States and to complement the National Fire Plan, which focuses more on tactics and implementation.

Zimmerman, G. Thomas; Bunnell, David L. 2000. The Federal Wildland Fire Policy: opportunities for wilderness fire management. In: Cole, David N.; McCool, Stephen F.; Borrie, William T.; O'Loughlin, Jennifer, comps. Proceedings: wilderness science in a time of change—Volume 5: wilderness ecosystems, threats, and management; 1999 May 23–27; Missoula, MT. Proc. RMRS-P-15-VOL-5. Ogden, UT: U.S. Department of Agriculture, Forest Service, Rocky Mountain Research Station: 288–298.

Annotation: This paper summarizes and discusses the 1995 Federal fire policy and its implications for wilderness fire management. The authors suggest that the 1995 policy enables more integrated planning, provides greater flexibility in funding, and offers more opportunities for the use of prescribed fire in Forest Service Wilderness areas. Based on an evaluation of the management of 1998 fires in the Northern Rocky Mountains, it appears that the 1995 policy is positively affecting the number of fires managed for resource benefits. The authors suggest that the new fire classification system, where all wildland fires are "appropriately managed," facilitates the use of a range of actions and no longer dichotomously classifies fires as either "wildfire" (to be suppressed) or "prescribed natural fire" (allowed to burn within specific bounds). The paper identifies a range of strategies for managing wildland fire and discusses the general conditions under which each is appropriate. Finally, future needs, which include proactive management, accommodation of uncertainty, and better documentation of management actions and their results, are identified.

2. Administrative Boundaries

Bunnell, David L.; Zimmerman, G. Thomas. 1998. Fire management in the North Fork of the Flathead River, Montana: an example of a fully integrated interagency fire management program. In: Pruden, Teresa L.; Brennan, Leonard A., eds. Fire in ecosystem management: shifting the paradigm from suppression to prescription; 1996 May 7–10; Boise, ID. Tall Timbers Fire Ecology Conference Proceedings, No. 20. Tallahassee, FL: Tall Timbers Research Station: 274–279.

Annotation: This paper describes how three resource management agencies, the National Park Service, U.S. Forest Service, and Montana Department of State Lands, are working together to manage fire in and around Glacier National Park. Despite differences in land management objectives, the agencies developed coordinated fire response plans that utilize multiple strategies: control, containment, confinement, prescribed burning, and prescribed natural fire. The authors illustrate the results of this integrated management program using the 1994 fire season as an example.

Desmond, Jim. 1994. Interagency wilderness fire management. In: Weise, David R.; Martin, Robert E., tech. coords. 1995. The Biswell symposium: fire issues and solutions in urban interface and wildland ecosystems; 1994 February 15–17; Walnut Creek, CA. Gen. Tech. Rep. PSW-GTR-158. Albany, CA: U.S. Department of Agriculture, Forest Service, Pacific Southwest Research Station: 51–54.

Annotation: This brief paper discusses coordination in managing wilderness fire across agency boundaries, emphasizing communication as a central factor in success. The process used to coordinate fire planning between National Parks and Forest Service wilderness areas in the Sierra Nevada is described.

Landres, Peter B.; Marsh, Susan; Merigliano, Linda; Ritter, Dan; Norman, Andy. 1998b. Boundary effects on wilderness and other natural areas. In: Knight, Richard L; Landres, Peter B., eds. Stewardship across boundaries. Washington, DC: Island Press: 117–140.

Annotation: This chapter discusses the ecological and social effects of boundaries on wilderness and natural areas and uses fire management as an example to illustrate how boundaries can alter ecological flows into and out of wilderness areas. Landres and others discuss the problems caused by incongruities between ecological and administrative boundaries and the consequences of boundaries for planning and management in wilderness. The chapter outlines two different models used in Federal wilderness management: the "wilderness separate" and the "wilderness similar" approaches. In the first case, wilderness is treated as a discrete and different area and planning occurs separately for wilderness and adjacent Federal lands. In the latter case, wilderness is viewed on a continuum with other lands and planning is integrated on a broader scale. The benefits and drawbacks of each approach are discussed.

Little, Ronda L.; Schonewald-Cox, Christine. 1990. Fire management policy and boundary effects on parks: Lassen Volcanic National Park—a case study. In: van Ripper, C.; Stohlgren, T. J.; Veirs, S. D.; Hillyer, S. C., eds. Examples of resource inventory and monitoring in National Parks of California, Proceedings of the third biennial conference on research in California's National Parks. Washington, DC: U.S. Department of the Interior, National Park Service: 249–256.

Annotation: This short paper uses the 1987 Snag Fire in Lassen Volcanic National Park to examine the effects of administrative boundaries on fire management. When spot fires moved too close to the park's perimeter, fire fighting began in order to protect timber on the adjacent Lassen National Forest. The authors used this information to delineate regions in the park where the Park Service has significant control over fire management versus those where fire management is heavily influenced by surrounding lands. They conclude that fire is allowed to burn naturally, without suppression, in only a small portion of the park.

Plevel, Steve R. 1997. Fire policy at the wildland-urban interface. Journal of Forestry. 95(10): 12–17.

Annotation: See annotation in section II.D.2, page 26.

3. Wildland-Urban Interface

Feary, Karen M.; Neuenschwander, Leon F. 1998. Predicting fire behavior in the wildland-urban interface. In: Pruden, Teresa L.; Brennan, Leonard A., eds. Fire in ecosystem management: shifting the paradigm from suppression to prescription; 1996 May 7–10; Boise, ID. Tall Timbers Fire Ecology Conference Proceedings, No. 20. Tallahassee, FL: Tall Timbers Research Station: 44–48.

Annotation: Although we typically associate wilderness with remoteness from urban influences or human habitation, wilderness management is increasingly influenced by home development at the edge of wildlands and wilderness fire policies may be substantially affected by wildland-urban interface issues. This brief article provides an overview of fire risk issues at the wildland-urban interface and suggests that GIS-based models can be used to map hazard areas, facilitating risk management. Barriers to managing fire risk are also discussed: challenges include zoning regulations, social attitudes, and insurance systems. A map-based modeling approach might help overcome some of these barriers by visually illustrating risks and facilitating landscape-scale planning. The paper's literature cited section includes a number of additional recent articles on fire at the urban-wildland interface, an issue that wilderness managers increasingly face as more people occupy lands adjacent to protected areas.

Fischer, William C.; Arno, Stephen F., comps. 1988. Protecting people and homes from wildfire in the Interior West: proceedings of the symposium and workshop; 1987 October 6–8; Missoula, MT. Gen. Tech. Rep. INT-251. Ogden, UT: U.S. Department of Agriculture, Forest Service, Intermountain Research Station. 213 p.

Annotation: In the West, developments at the edge of wildlands have begun to have a substantial affect on fire management on Federal lands, including wilderness. This symposium focuses on fire at the wildland/urban interface in the Western United States, though many of the papers provide information and ideas that should be relevant to other regions as well. A number of contributions emphasize communication strategies among homeowners, developers, politicians, land managers, and the media. Other papers discuss how to integrate wildland fire management at the national, state, and local levels. Additionally, the proceedings includes discussions of land use planning, building design, landscaping and other techniques to control fire in residential areas in and near wildlands.

Plevel, Steve R. 1997. Fire policy at the wildland-urban interface. Journal of Forestry. 95(10): 12–17.

Annotation: See annotation in section II.D.2, page 26.

Weise, David R.; Martin, Robert E., tech. coords. 1995. The Biswell symposium: fire issues and solutions in urban interface and wildland ecosystems; 1994 February 15–17; Walnut Creek, CA. Gen. Tech. Rep. PSW-GTR-158. Albany, CA: U.S. Department of Agriculture, Forest Service, Pacific Southwest Research Station. 199 p.

Annotation: Although wilderness fire management did not play a central role in the discussions at this symposium, many of the topics are relevant to fire management in wilderness areas that are small or abut private lands. This fire management symposium centers on wildland-urban interface issues. A discussion of the California's 1991 Oakland-Berkeley Hills fire, in which both lives and property were lost, leads off and serves as a focal point for the symposium, although the papers range widely. The symposium includes articles on barriers to prescribed fire and fuel management, agency objectives in relation to wildland fire management, urban interface strategies and policies, and other topics relating to the resolution of conflicts posed by the natural process of fire and human needs for safety, clean air, and places to live.

4. Large Fires and High-Intensity Fires

Heinselman, Miron L. 1985. Fire regimes and management options in ecosystems with large high-intensity fires. In: Lotan, James E.; Kilgore, Bruce M.; Fischer, William C.; Mutch, Robert W., eds. Proceedings—symposium and workshop on wilderness fire; 1983 November 15–18; Missoula, MT. Gen. Tech. Rep. INT-182. Ogden, UT: U.S. Department of Agriculture, Forest Service, Intermountain Forest and Range Experiment Station: 81–86.

Annotation: In this paper, Heinselman describes patterns of large and high-intensity fires in a number of different wilderness ecosystems: the boreal forest, the Great-Lakes-Acadian ecosystem, the Rocky Mountains, and the Douglas-fir region of the Pacific Northwest. After explaining regional differences, the author examines the relationships between fuels, stand age, and time since last fire. These relationships vary from region to region, therefore local fire histories and an understanding of local fire regimes play an important role in wilderness fire planning. The last section of the paper focuses on management options for large and high-intensity fires, emphasizing the importance of safety, identifying factors that affect wilderness managers' freedom to allow large fires to burn, and evaluating the roles of natural fire, prescribed burning, and fire suppression in wilderness.

Turner, Monica G.; Hargrove, William W.; Gardner, Robert H.; Romme, William H. 1994. Effects of fire on landscape heterogeneity in Yellowstone National Park, Wyoming. Journal of Vegetation Science. 5:731–742.

Annotation: This study examined the patterns of fire intensity and the isolation of burned areas created by the large fires of 1988 in Yellowstone National Park. Even in areas with large fires, the authors found that burn intensity varied, and most crown fires were less than 200 m from an unburned "green edge." These results suggest that even large patches of burned forest are within range of seed sources for regeneration. Management implications are discussed.

van Wagtendonk, Jan W. 1995. Large fires in wilderness areas. In: Brown, James K.; Mutch, Robert W.; Spoon, Charles W.; Wakimoto, Ronald H., tech. coords. 1995. Proceedings: symposium on fire in wilderness and park management; 1993 March 30–April 1; Missoula, MT. Gen. Tech. Rep. INT-GTR-320. Ogden, UT: U.S. Department of Agriculture, Forest Service, Intermountain Research Station: 113–116.

Annotation: In this paper, van Wagtendonk discusses considerations for prescribed natural fire in wilderness and protected areas, using Yosemite National Park as an example. In addition to understanding the "natural" role of fire in a particular ecosystem, managers need to take into account the risk of fire spread beyond areas boundaries, smoke and air quality concerns, safety, and the availability of fire fighting personnel. After appropriate fire management plans are developed and implemented, fire patterns can be compared to historic fire regimes to evaluate program success.

5. Mechanical Thinning

Heinlein, Thomas A.; Covington, W. Wallace; Fule, Peter Z.; Moore, Margaret M.; Smith, Hiram B. 2000. Development of ecological restoration experiments in Grand Canyon National Park. In: Cole, David N.; McCool, Stephen F.; Borrie, William T.; O'Loughlin, Jennifer, comps. Wilderness science in a time of change conference—Volume 5: wilderness ecosystems, threats, and management; 1999 May 23–27; Missoula, MT. Proc. RMRS-P-15-VOL-5. Ogden, UT: U.S. Department of Agriculture, Forest Service, Rocky Mountain Research Station: 249–254.

Annotation: "Process restoration"— using prescribed burning and appropriately managing natural fires—has been used to reintroduce fire to many U.S. protected areas. However, the authors assert that in certain forest types, "structural restoration," involving mechanical thinning, may be more effective than process restoration in restoring forest structure, preventing adverse ecological effects, and enabling the return of fire as a natural process. In the Grand Canyon, for example, prescribed fires may burn intensely due to fuel buildups under fire suppression, with consequences that differ from historic fire effects and potentially impact native species. Heinlein and others suggest that mechanical thinning may circumvent such undesired consequences, though they acknowledge the controversy surrounding the use of such interventions in protected areas. The authors argue that careful research can help elucidate the advantages and disadvantages of different restoration techniques, and they describe an experimental study on the North and South Rims of the Grand Canyon examining four different restoration treatments (including prescribed fire, thinning, and a combination of these techniques) and their effects on forest structure and species composition.

Miller, Carol; Urban, Dean L. 2000. Modeling the effects of fire management alternatives on Sierra Nevada mixed-conifer forests. Ecological Applications. 10(1): 85–94.

Annotation: See annotation in section II.C.2, page 23.

Stephenson, Nathan L. 1999. Reference conditions for giant sequoia restoration: structure, process, and precision. Ecological Applications. 9(4): 1253–1265.

Annotation: See annotation in section II.C.2, page 24.

van Wagtendonk, Jan W. 1996. Use of a deterministic fire growth model test fuel treatments. In: Sierra Nevada Ecosystem Project: final report to Congress, Vol. II, Assessments and scientific basis for management options. Davis, CA: University of California, Centers for Water and Wildland Resources: 1155–1165.

Annotation: See annotation in section II.C.2, page 24.

6. Fire and Climate

Grissino-Mayer, Henri D.; Swetnam, Thomas W. 2000. Century-scale climate forcing of fire regimes in the American Southwest. The Holocene. 10(2): 213–220.

Annotation: In this paper, Grissino-Mayer and Swetnam report the results of a 1,000-year reconstruction of fire and precipitation in northwestern New Mexico. The authors found significant changes in fire frequency, fire spread, and fire seasonality on century scales as well as changes in the relationship between precipitation and fire. Data suggest that climate and fire are interrelated in complex ways: for example, above average rainfall may increase fuel accumulation and increase fires in dry years. The authors conclude that climate changes will likely alter global fire regimes. However the nature of the changes will depend on patterns of temperature and precipitation and their interaction with the biotic environment.

Kipfmueller, Kurt F.; Swetnam, Thomas W. 2000. Fire-climate interactions in the Selway-Bitterroot Wilderness Area. In: Cole, David N.; McCool, Stephen F.; Borrie, William T.; O'Loughlin, Jennifer, comps. Wilderness science in a time of change conference—Volume 5: Wilderness ecosystems, threats, and management; 1999 May 23–27; Missoula, MT. Proc. RMRS-P-15-VOL-5. Ogden, UT: U.S. Department of Agriculture, Forest Service, Rocky Mountain Research Station: 270–275.

Annotation: This study shows a relationship between climate and fire in the Selway-Bitterroot Wilderness. The authors found that fire years occurred when summers were significantly drier than average, and fires tended to follow a wet year 4 years previous. The authors suggest that the relationships between climate and fire could be further elucidated if individual forest types were studied and compared.

Millar, Constance I.; Woolfenden, Wallace B. 1999. The role of climate change in interpreting historical variability. Ecological Applications. 9(4): 1207–1216.

Annotation: Without considering changes in climate, historical variability may be misinterpreted and misapplied in ecological restoration, Millar and Woolfenden assert in this paper. The authors describe how climate has shifted from the Middle Ages to today and discuss the interrelationships between climate, vegetation, and ecological processes. Implications of climate changes for ecosystem management are then discussed in the context of two case studies, one from California's Mono Lake, and the other from a forested roadless area in the Sierra Nevada Mountains. Millar and Woolfenden conclude with a number of considerations for management, including the admonition that attempting to reconstruct the past may be both inappropriate and infeasible in light of differences between present and past climates.

Ryan, Kevin C. 1991. Vegetation and wildland fire: implications of global climate change. Environment International. 17: 169–178.

Annotation: In this paper, Ryan outlines the causes and potential consequences of global climate change in relation to wildland fire. Although substantial uncertainty remains in our understanding of global climate change on planetary, regional, and local scales, models suggest that with a doubling of carbon dioxide, mean global temperature will rise 4 °C and precipitation at mid-latitudes will decrease, while precipitation and low and high latitudes will increase. In temperate forests, global climate change may increase the frequency and severity of fire. The complex interactions between vegetation, fire, and climate are discussed, and Ryan outlines important social and philosophical issues related to the management of fire in light of global change. Ryan specifically identifies a number of questions relevant to wilderness fire management under a changing climate.

Swetnam, Thomas W. 1993. Fire history and climate change in giant sequoia groves. Science. 262: 885–889.

Annotation: In this paper, Swetnam discusses the results of a 2,000-year reconstruction of fire history and climate for five giant sequoia groves in California. Fire occurrence in the five groves was more synchronous than would be expected if fires were controlled by local factors; Swetnam argues therefore that regional climatic conditions may exert some control over fire occurrence. Additionally, fire occurrence was related to precipitation at annual time scales, and to temperature at decadal and century scales. Swetnam discusses the interaction of factors at multiple scales in controlling fire regimes, and suggests that nonequilibrium conditions influence fire, whose patterns change constantly over time in response to climate and other factors.

Torn, Margaret S.; Fried, Jeremy S. 1992. Predicting the impacts of global warming on wildland fire. Climatic Change. 21: 257–274.

Annotation: This paper presents the results of a modeling study focused on the interactions between climate change and fire. Because climate predictions are uncertain, and fire behavior models focus at different spatial and temporal scales than the general circulation models used to simulate climate change, little is known about how fire and climate interact. In this study, Torn and Fried used an integrated model to examine fire and climate processes in northern California, finding that increases in both temperature and wind resulted in greater fire intensity, more escaped fires, and a larger area burned. The authors discuss the implications of their results for understanding fire and climate more generally and identify gaps in data needed for modeling. Although wilderness fire managers are unlikely to have any direct control over factors affecting climate change, understanding the potential implications of such change may assist managers in planning fire programs for the future.

Wotton, B. M.; Flannigan, M. D. 1993. Length of the fire season in a changing climate. The Forestry Chronicle. 69(2): 187–192.

Annotation: This study used global circulation models to examine potential changes in fire season length under increased carbon dioxide conditions and associated global climate change. In all regions of Canada, the model predicted an earlier start date and a later end date to the fire season, with an average predicted increase of 22 percent in the fire season length for Canada as a whole. Although these results may not be directly applicable to the United States—particularly for southern regions—they highlight a potential effect of climate change on fire regimes and the study utilizes a methodology that may be useful elsewhere.

7. Air Pollution From Wildland Fires

Brown, James K.; Bradshaw, Larry S. 1994. Comparisons of particulate emissions and smoke impacts from presettlement, full suppression, and prescribed natural fire periods in the Selway-Bitterroot Wilderness. International Journal of Wildland Fire. 4(3): 143–155.

Annotation: See annotation in section II.D.2, page 26.

Core, John E. 1997. Air quality regulations: treatment of emissions from wildfires vs. prescribed fires. In: Bryan, D. C., ed. Conference proceedings: environmental regulation and prescribed fire: legal and social challenges; 1995 March 14-17; Tampa Airport Hilton at MetroCenter, Tampa, FL. Tallahassee, FL: Florida State University, Center for Professional Development: 53–62.

Annotation: See annotation in section II.D.1, page 25.

Leenhouts, Bill. 1997. Presettlement fire and emission production estimates: a framework for understanding potential system change. In: Bryan, D. C., ed. Conference proceedings—environmental regulation and prescribed fire: legal and social challenges. Tallahassee, FL: Florida State University, Center for Professional Development: 236–241.

Annotation: Though very brief, this article estimates and compares current and historical atmospheric emissions from wildland fires across the United States. According to Leenhout's estimates, contemporary emissions from wildland fire are at approximately one-tenth of their presettlement levels. Leenhouts suggests that these and similar estimates can be used as a baseline in understanding fire's current role in ecosystems as compared to their historic effects.

McMahon, Charles K. 1999. Forest fires and smoke—impacts on air quality and human health in the U.S.A. Proceedings, TAPPI International Environmental Conference; 1999 April 18–21; Nashville, TN. Nashville, TN: TAPPI Press: 443–453. Available: http://www.srs.fs fed.us/pubs/ja/ja_mcmahon001.pdf [2001, June 5].

Annotation: This article traces the evolution of national air quality regulations and their relation to wildland fires. The paper outlines the structure of current Clean Air Act regulations and discusses the EPA's 1998 interim air quality policy on wildland and prescribed fires. The need for interagency collaboration, public education, and integrated Smoke Management Plans for wildland fires is discussed. The references section contains links to the EPA fire working group and the Western States Air Resource Council Web sites.

Procter, Trent. 1995. Working to make the Clean Air Act and prescribed burning compatible. In: Weise, David R.; Martin, Robert E., tech. coords. The Biswell symposium: fire issues and solutions in urban interface and wildland ecosystems; 1994 February 15-17; Walnut Creek, CA. Gen. Tech. Rep. PSW-GTR-158. Albany, CA: U.S. Department of Agriculture, Forest Service, Pacific Southwest Research Station: 125–128.

Annotation: See annotation in section II.D.1, page 25.

Sampson, R. Neil; Atkinson, R. Dwight; Lewis, Joe W. 2000. Mapping wildfire hazards and risks. [Co-published simultaneously as Journal of Sustainable Forestry, volume 11, numbers 1/2 2000.] New York: Food Products Press. 328 p.

Annotation: See annotation in section II.E, page 28.

U.S. Environmental Protection Agency. 1998. Interim air quality policy on wildland and prescribed fires, [Online]. Available: http://www.epa.gov/ttn/oarpg/t1/memoranda/firefnl.pdf [2001, June 5].

Annotation: This document outlines Federal policy on air quality and wildland fire. The requirements for Clean Air Act compliance are discussed, emphasizing the role of Smoke Management Plans. The need for collaboration among Federal land managers, Indian land managers, private land owners, air quality managers, and state and local governments is stressed, and roles for each of these groups are outlined. The policy addresses air quality compliance in the context of Federal wildland fire policy and recognizes the importance of wildland fire use as well as the need to protect airsheds for health and aesthetic reasons.

Western States Air Resource Council (WESTAR), [Online]. Available: http://www.westar.org/ [2001, June 5].

Annotation: This Website is the homepage of WESTAR, a cooperative air quality organization composed of 15 states and a number of Federal partners. WESTAR aims to "promote the exchange of information related to the control of air pollution for use in state and Federal activities as authorized by air quality statutes and regulations" and to work with Federal land managers and the EPA to develop strategies for maintaining air quality and protecting the environment. The site contains information on WESTAR air quality training sessions and work groups, as well as links to air quality programs in member states and to Federal air quality-related sites.

III. Additional Resources

A. Fire Management Plans

Because many wilderness fire plans were under revision at the time this reading list was compiled, we were unable to include sample fire management plans representing a diverse set of regions and agencies. However, we have included two Forest Service wilderness fire management plans that illustrate the types of issues, considerations, and management guidelines that fire plans can address. Fire plans will vary across agencies and administrative units depending on particular management directives and ecological and social characteristics. Additionally, the plans listed here will undergo revision as policies and conditions change.

U.S. Department of Agriculture, Forest Service, Bitterroot, Clearwater, Lolo and Nez Perce National Forests. 1997. Selway-Bitterroot fire management guidebook.

Annotation: This guidebook serves as the fire management plan for the Selway-Bitterroot Wilderness (SBW). The SBW has one of the longest running natural fire management programs in the country. The guidebook begins with a discussion of wilderness and general fire management objectives described in the Forest Service Manual. The document next describes the SBW and the characteristics of specific management units, then explains in detail procedures for conducting an initial decision analysis, developing a burn plan, and assessing ongoing fires. Additionally, annual monitoring and long-term program evaluation are discussed. Appendices focus on risk management, research natural areas, site and structure evaluation and protection, a public information plan, and skills and qualifications for fire management.

U.S. Department of Agriculture, Forest Service, Intermountain Region, Bridger Teton National Forest. 1996. Gros Ventre fire program: background and fire management plan. 72 p.

Annotation: This fire plan describes the context and management direction for fire in the Bridger Teton National Forest's Gros Ventre Wilderness. The Gros Ventre fire program aims "to maintain or restore fire to its natural role in the wilderness ecosystem and maintain a natural regime that operates with minimal human interference." The fire management plan provides background on the area's climate, weather, vegetation, and vegetation responses to fire. Additionally, fire history, fuel characteristics, and fire regimes are described. The plan delineates three management zones and identifies the responsibilities of line, wilderness, and fire management officers with regard to wilderness fire. Procedures for managing prescribed natural fires, management ignitions, and wildfires are outlined in detail, and the plan pays particular attention to minimizing fire suppression impacts in wilderness.

B. Online Resources

This section lists a number of Web sites and online documents relevant to fire ecology and management. The U.S. Forest Service, Bureau of Land Management, National Park Service, and Fish and Wildlife Service all maintain fire-related Web sites, which are included here. Additionally a number of online bibliographies and databases are cited: the most comprehensive of these are the fire ecology database maintained by Tall Timbers Research Station and the Fire Effects Information System developed by the U.S. Forest Service's Rocky Mountain Research Station. Finally, we provide links for policy documents, such as the 1995 Federal Wildland Fire Policy and the Environmental Protection Agency's Interim Policy on Wildland and Prescribed Fires, that bear on wilderness fire management and restoration. Brief annotations for these sites highlight the information most relevant to wilderness fire restoration; for some sites, longer annotations in sections I and II of the reading list are cited. Each citation in this section is followed by the date we last accessed the homepage.

Aldo Leopold Wilderness Research Institute, [Online]. Available: http://www.wilderness net/leopold [2001, June 5].

Annotation: This site is the homepage of the Leopold Institute, a Federal interagency research group that provides scientific leadership to sustain wilderness. The Leopold Institute has identified natural disturbances, including wilderness fire, as one of its three priority research issues. This reading list as well others in the Linking Wilderness Research and Management Series are available online.

Bibliography of Fire Effects and Related Literature— Applicable to the Ecosystems and Species of Wisconsin, [Online]. Available: http://www npwrc.usgs.gov/resource/literatr/firebibl/firebibl.htm [2001, June 1].

Annotation: This downloadable bibliography contains more than 800 citations on fire effects in the Midwestern United States.

Bureau of Land Management National Office of Fire and Aviation, [Online]. Available: http://www fire.blm.gov/ [2001, June 1].

Annotation: This site contains current fire information for BLM lands, fire policy documents, fire statistics, links to fire research, and links to other relevant agency sites, such as the National Interagency Fire Center.

Fire Information Cache: Sequoia-Kings Canyon National Parks, [Online]. Available: http://www.nps.gov.seki/fire/indxfire htm [2001, May 31].

Annotation: This site houses the fire management plan for Sequoia and Kings Canyon National Parks, National Park Service fire policy information, online fire research papers, research project information, and a fire bibliography (available: http://www.nps.gov/seki/fire/fire_bib htm), divided into three sections: General Literature, Technical and Scientific Literature, and Historic and Background Literature. The bibliography emphasizes literature relevant to the Sierra Nevada region.

Fire Information Systems Online, [Online]. Available: http://www fire.org [2001, June 1].

Annotation: This is a central site for accessing and downloading fire behavior simulation models. Contains direct links to the Fire Effects Information System (FEIS), the Citation Retrieval System (a searchable database of all sources used to create the FEIS), and Fire Management Tools Online. Links to U.S. Forest Service fire information and other related sites are also included.

The International Fire Information Network, [Online]. Available: http://www.csu.edu.au/firenet/ [2001, June 1].

Annotation: This site is a "Special Interest Network dedicated to all aspects of fire science and management." It includes a virtual library, as well as information on "fire behaviour, fire weather…plant and animal responses to fire and all aspects of fire effects."

Kirby, Ronald E.; Lewis, Stephen J.; Sexson, Terry N. (1998, April). Fire in North American wetland ecosystems and fire-wildlife relations: an annotated bibliography, [Online]. U.S. Fish and Wildlife Service Biological Report 88(1). Available: http://www.npwrc.usgs.gov/resource/literatr/firewild/firewild.htm [2001, May 31].

Annotation: This searchable bibliography contains more than 300 citations related to fire effects on wildlife in wetland ecosystems.

National Interagency Fire Center, [Online]. Available: http://www.nifc.gov [2001, May 31].

Annotation: This site offers current wildland fire information, national interagency coordination center reports, fire prevention and education information, science and technology information related to fire, National Fire Plan information, a link to the 2001 Review and Update of the 1995 Federal Wildland Fire Policy, and links to individual agency fire sites.

National Park Service FireNet, [Online]. Available: http://www.nps.gov/fire [2001, May 31].

Annotation: This site provides fire policy, science, planning, safety and employment information for the National Park Service. It includes information on wildland fire, including relevant science; the National Park Service Implementation Strategy for the National Fire Plan; fire at the wildland-urban interface; fire prevention and education; and current fire information.

National Wildfire Coordinating Group, [Online]. Available: http://www.nwcg.gov/teams/wfewt/NWCGBib/fireecology.html [2001, May 31].

Annotation: This site lists a variety of Web sites with fire ecology information.

Tall Timbers Research Station E. V. Komarek Fire Ecology Database, [Online]. Available: http://www.talltimbers.org/feco.html [2001, May 31].

Annotation: An extensive, keyword-searchable database with over 10,800 publications related to fire ecology. The bibliography emphasizes the United States, and particularly the Southeastern United States. However, international papers are included as well. The bibliography is updated frequently and is easy to use.

U.S. Department of Agriculture, Forest Service, Rocky Mountain Research Station, Fire Sciences Laboratory (2001, May). Fire Effects Information System, [Online]. Available: http://www.fs.fed.us/database/feis/ [2001, June 1].

Annotation: This searchable database provides synopses of fire effects on individual plant and animal species. The database also includes summaries of fire effects on plant communities of North America (by Kuchler vegetation type). For each species or community type, a bibliography lists full citations of source material.

U.S. Department of the Interior; U.S. Department of Agriculture. 1995. Federal wildland fire management policy and program review, [Online]. Available: http://www fs.fed.us/land/wdfirex htm [2001, June 5].

Annotation: This policy document was updated with the 2001 Review and Update of the 1995 Federal Wildland Fire Management Policy (see annotation in section II.F.1, page 30); however, the 2001 review affirms that the policy's principles remain central guideposts for wildland fire management.

U.S. Environmental Protection Agency. 1998. Interim air quality policy on wildland and prescribed fires [Online]. Available: http://www.epa.gov/ttn/oarpg/t1/memoranda/firefnl.pdf [2001, June 5].

Annotation: See annotation in section II.F.7, page 34.

U.S. Fish and Wildlife Service Fire Management, [Online]. Available: http://fire.r9.fws.gov [2001, May 31].

Annotation: A repository of information on U.S. Fish and Wildlife Service fire policy and guidance, prescribed fire, and wildland fire monitoring. Contains links to interagency fire research, the USFWS Fire Management Handbook (requires password for access), and daily fire situation reports.

U.S. Forest Service Fire Page, [Online]. Available: http://www.fs fed.us/land/#fire [2001, May 31].

Annotation: Contains links to fire systems and data, fire news and publications, fire research centers, and fire policy documents.

U.S. Forest Service Fire and Aviation Site, [Online]. Available: http://www.fs.fed.us/fire/ [2001, May 31].

Annotation: Contains U.S. Forest Service fire policy, science, planning, safety, and employment information. Includes links to the Forest Service National Fire Plan, policy information, agency fire research, and the publication Fire Management Today (formerly Fire Management Notes).

Western States Air Resource Council (WESTAR) [Online]. Available: http://www.westar.org/ [2001, June 5].

Annotation: See annotation in section II.F.7, page 34.

www.fire.org. (2000, July 10—last update). Available: http://www.fire.org [2001, June 1].

Annotation: This site offers links to downloadable fire simulation models and other online resources. See annotation in section I.B1, page 7.

AUTHOR INDEX

Multiple page number listings result from works cited in more than one section of the document. For articles that appear more than once, an * marks the page containing the annotation.

Rocky Mountain Research Station
240 West Prospect Road
Fort Collins, CO 80526

RMRS
ROCKY MOUNTAIN RESEARCH STATION

The Rocky Mountain Research Station develops scientific information and technology to improve management, protection, and use of the forests and rangelands. Research is designed to meet the needs of National Forest managers, Federal and State agencies, public and private organizations, academic institutions, industry, and individuals.

Studies accelerate solutions to problems involving ecosystems, range, forests, water, recreation, fire, resource inventory, land reclamation, community sustainability, forest engineering technology, multiple use economics, wildlife and fish habitat, and forest insects and diseases. Studies are conducted cooperatively, and applications may be found worldwide.

Research Locations

Flagstaff, Arizona	Reno, Nevada
Fort Collins, Colorado*	Albuquerque, New Mexico
Boise, Idaho	Rapid City, South Dakota
Moscow, Idaho	Logan, Utah
Bozeman,Montana	Ogden, Utah
Missoula, Montana	Provo, Utah
Lincoln, Nebraska	Laramie, Wyoming

*Station Headquarters, Natural Resources Research Center, 2150 Centre Avenue, Building A, Fort Collins, CO 80526